A Bite-Sized Public Affairs Book

What's the Point of Ofcom?

Edited by

John Mair

Cover by

Dean Stockton

Published by Bite-Sized Books Ltd 2021
©John Mair 2021

BITE-SIZED BOOKS

Bite-Sized Books Ltd Cleeve Road, Goring RG8 9BJ UK

information@bite-sizedbooks.com

Registered in the UK. Company Registration No: 9395379

ISBN: 9798742003441

The moral right of John Mair to be identified as the author of this work has been asserted by him in accordance with the Copyright, Designs and Patents Act 1988

Although the publisher, editors and authors have used reasonable care in preparing this book, the information it contains is distributed as is and without warranties of any kind. This book is not intended as legal, financial, social or technical advice and not all recommendations may be suitable for your situation. Professional advisors should be consulted as needed. Neither the publisher nor the author shall be liable for any costs, expenses or damages resulting from use of or reliance on the information contained in this book.

Contents

Overview: The Big Questions

Introduction — 2
John Mair

Chapter One — 4

Ofcom and Me: A Job application

Rt.Hon Sir Alan Moses, Judge, Former Head Independent Press Standards Organisation

Chapter Two — 10

Can Ofcom pull off the political/technocratic confidence trick?

Bill Emmott, Former Editor *The Economist*, Former Chair *Ofcom* Content Board

Chapter Three — 18

Has Ofcom forgotten its roots?

Steve Barnett, Professor of Communications, University of Westminster

Chapter Four — 26

Regulating the Titans and Free Speech

Mark Thompson, Former BBC DG/New York Times CEO

Chapter Five — 31

The US shows us why we need Ofcom

Clive Myrie, Royal Television Society Journalist of the Year 2021

Section One
A Watchdog With Teeth...Or Just Gums?

Introduction   37
    John Mair

Chapter Six   39
    A (not so)brief history of PSB Time
      David Elstein Former Senior Executive Thames, Sky Television, Channel Five.

Chapter Seven   53
    Ofcom: In the beginning
      Janice Hughes CBE Graphite Strategy. Early Oftel/Ofcom strategist.

Chapter Eight   60
    Time for Ofcom to re-visit and re-invent Granada-land
      Simon Albury MBE, Former CEO The Royal Television Society.

Chapter Nine   67
    Just what does Ofcom mean by Diversity?
      Marcus Ryder MBE, Diversity Champion.

Chapter Ten   73
    Ofcom: a Naked Attraction to liberals?
      Robin Aitken MBE, *Daily Telegraph* **columnist.**

SECTION TWO
TAMING THE TIGER? REGULATING THE BBC

Introduction   79
    John Mair

Chapter Eleven   80
    Regulating the BBC: Notes from the front-line
    Jacquie Hughes, Former *Ofcom* executive.

Chapter Twelve   86
    Is the BBC and Broadcast Journalism at the Frontline of a Culture War
    Peter Jukes, *Byline Times*.

SECTION THREE
PRIORITIES FOR THE NEW CHAIR

Introduction   92
    John Mair

Chapter Thirteen   94
    The Ides of March for Piers
    Paul Connew, Former Editor *Sunday Mirror*/Media commentator.

Chapter Fourteen   100
    Why NOT to make Paul Dacre the story rather than a regulator
    Phillip Collins, former Chief speech writer for Tony Blair/Columnist at *The Times*.

Chapter Fifteen   **104**

> *Paul Dacre, Ofcom and the Coming of the Post-Nolan Era*
>
> > **Julian Petley, Professor of Journalism, Brunel University.**

Chapter Sixteen   **110**

> *Ofcom: Firmly a bystander to history in television and in telephony*
>
> > **Christopher Williams, *Telegraph* Business Editor.**

Acknowledgements

As ever these Mair 'Hackademic' books (this is the 39th) owe it all to the authors. They are recruited, usually willingly, to lend of their experience for no fee and in a VERY strict timetable. Most have been uncomplaining, all (bar one or two) have delivered, nearly all reacted well to editorial chivvying and suggestions.

This book, to the best of my knowledge is the first tome about our most important regulator in UK as it enters uncharted waters with regulation on on-line harms and through them the tech mega-titans.

Plus there is the 'D' question-just who will be the new chair. Interviews are currently taking place with the new supremo announced in May. He or she could change the cultural landscape of Britain beyond retrieval.

Thanks to the publishers-Paul Davies and new CEO of Bite-Sized Books Julian Costley whom I knew in a previous life. As ever Dean Stockton has delivered a brilliant cover .And to the long-suffering Susan my wife who has lived with me taking over the dining table to work.

As to the contents and tone, I leave that to your judgement.

John Mair Oxford England. Easter Sunday 2021

General Introduction – The Big Questions

John Mair

Ofcom is one of the key regulators in twenty first century Britain. It supervises the big industries of the present and the future: telephony, broadcasting, media, and so on. It is at the intersection of technology, culture and politics. *Ofcom* is also at its own crossroads with a new chair to be announced in late Spring 2021. That individual could shape the public sphere for decades to come. Hence, this book – the first to my knowledge about the regulator – simply asks what is the point of *Ofcom*? And is it fit for purpose after close to two decades of existence?

A panoply of those with knowledge and experience cast their minds to these big questions.

First, an overview from some big beasts. None more so than the Right Honourable Sir Alan Moses. For five years he was the 'regulator' for the printed word in the UK: the Independent Press Standards Organisation. The Johnson government has announced that they are looking for a new chair for *Ofcom*. Sir Alan has decided to apply, partly tongue-in-cheek, in '***Ofcom* and Me: A Job application**'. He covers his experience as a regulator, but also asks whether broadcasting needs regulation at all. He is not expected to make the short list.

Bill Emmott worked for *Ofcom* for five months in 2016. The former Editor in Chief of *the Economist* was Head of the *Ofcom* Content Board as well as being on the main Executive Board. He fell out with the Chair and CEO as a result of the political echo from the Brexit referendum and was sacked as a result. After going to judicial review, he won his case and costs. In '**Can *Ofcom* pull off the political/technocratic confidence trick?**' Emmott thinks *Ofcom* has been pulling off an uneasy balance between politics, technology, and content regulation from the start and most especially since it took over supervision of the BBC in 2017. In his words 'the elastic has snapped'.

Professor Steven Barnett of the University of Westminster is a veteran observer of the British media scene. He goes back to the roots and revisits the battles at the turn of the century over the legislation which set up *Ofcom*. Who was it to serve? Citizens? Customers? The tech/broadcasting industries? In his view, *Ofcom* has torn up these long fought for roots – especially since taking on BBC responsibility post-2017?

There are fewer bigger beasts in the world media jungle than Mark Thompson. A former successful Director General of the BBC, before that the CEO of *Channel Four*, he has since crossed the Atlantic to transform the fortunes of the *New York Times* as President and CEO. In his Philip Geddes Memorial **Lecture 'The Lie in the Machine: Big tech and the limits of free speech'** he looks at the social media undercurrents leading to the Capitol insurrection last January, as well as the role of QAnon and the ways in which old style broadcast regulation may be applied to the internet. He comes to a surprising conclusion.

The final chapter is from one of the great current TV reporters, Clive Myrie of BBC News. A double award winner this year at the RTS journalism awards, Clive is a former BBC Correspondent in the US and has reported extensively from there. In his March lecture in honour of Harold Evans (curated and produced by me) **'Over here, over there: Why the US News Jungle shows just why we need broadcast regulation in the UK'**, Myrie draws on recent (and past) experiences of partisan US television to come down firmly in favour of impartiality and content regulation.

Let the debate about the new chair and the future of this most important gatekeeper to quality in our cultural and public life begin in earnest.

Chapter One

Ofcom and Me: A Job application

> Applications for the job of Chair of *Ofcom* are about to close. Just in time, one has come in from The Rt. Hon. Sir Alan Moses, former regulator and Court of Appeal judge.

There must be more curious ambitions but there are few more eccentric than wanting to be a regulator. It was not something to which I aspired. What could the attraction be in a whipping post which allowed others to vent their frustration, anger, disappointment and pomposity? The regulated constantly complain at the regulator's tendency to overstep the mark, whilst never condescending to explain where the mark is and those for whose benefit the regulatory system has been put in place cry out at the feeble and pusillanimous attempts of the regulator to provide protection or redress. But as we wait with breath ever so slightly bated to hear who is to be the next Chair of *Ofcom,* a twinge of disappointment creeps up on me. Is it too late for me to apply? To have the chance to regulate the BBC strikes me as a worthy ambition. Let me explain.

My previous life as a regulator

I did become a regulator, the first chairman of a new press regulator, the Independent Press Standards Organisation, (IPSO), determined to be different from the PCC. I remained for five years. I loved some minutes of it. Young, bright and intelligent staff dealt with the anguish of the public with care and sympathy. But few of my misgivings were allayed. It seemed so complicated and so unlike the austere simplicity of my previous job over a period of 18 years, as a judge. Judges have the great good fortune to have the authority of the law thrust upon them; the punters, litigants, advocates, newspaper editors (a surprising number of them) bow and scrape and above all laugh at their jokes. It matters not whether the judgments are good, bad or indifferent, nor that most are far too long and repetitive. If you win, the judge is a pillar of justice and his judgment seminal and luminous; if you lose, he is an 'enemy of the people' or was asleep. The authority he wields (and it is still a predominantly masculine authority) does not come from the excellence of his analysis, but from the status of his position. Indeed, respect for a judge which depends on the quality of his judgment is the antithesis of *authority* or *the rule of law*. Above all judges can make people do what they say. How different the life of a regulator. Nobody laughs at their jokes.

The Naked regulator

Most regulators have no built-in authority, there is nothing about them which inherently commands respect. Some regulators, of course, like those who regulate most of the professions, have, as their source of authority, statutory powers and can impose statutory obligations which have the force of law. Typically, the regulated are compelled to obey as a condition of entry to a particular profession and to avoid breaches of the rules of conduct to prevent expulsion. IPSO had no statutory base, it was created by the regulated, the press. This was, to those who spent too little time to think about it, a cause of criticism; self-regulation is always open to the accusation of self-interest, that it is little more than a sop to those who seek protection. But those critics never faced the only practical alternative, a system of statutory licensing.

Licensing the press, last mooted by Prime Minister John Major in the early 70s and so *sotto voce* a threat in the Leveson Report as to be difficult to hear, has ever remained true to Milton's description that it would be like a farmer erecting a gate to keep the crows from his field.

But self-regulation always remained, at least in my time, discomforting for a regulator who seeks to establish independence but is dependent on the acquiescence of the regulated. In relation to the press, the legal obligations which underpinned the regulations were derived from the willingness of the press to sign a contract with the regulator.

After Leveson, most of the national and regional press had reached the view that to avoid some more severe but unspecified method of control it was necessary to create a system of self-regulation. They appreciated that to do so, the system could not, as it had always been in the past, entirely voluntary. It was necessary to confer legal power on a regulator to impose obligations which the regulated press was required to obey. The mechanism by which that was achieved was a contract which conferred power on IPSO to respond to complaints, to make decisions as to whether breaches had occurred and to impose sanctions in the case of a breach. The regulated were required, under the contract they had signed, to co-operate, and to comply with rulings.

Did IPSO fail?

The great failure of IPSO, or to be honest, I fear, my failure, was a failure of persuasion. I never was able to convince those few who were interested in press regulation that self-regulation was anything other than self-interest. Freed from the pervasive clichés of those who criticised, such as *they're marking their own papers,* or *the last chance saloon*, there was an essential truth in the accusation that the system was motivated by self-interest. So it is, but the question too rarely asked was whether that was necessarily a bad thing. It was all too easily assumed that because it was self-interest which triggered the intention to set up a system of regulation, such regulation was doomed to failure and should be derided and condemned.

Such an automatic response ignored some fundamental aspects of any system of regulation. Self-interest is a vital ingredient for such a system to be...I was about to write "successful", though that is a concept too chimerical to be of any use. I often pondered on what the correct answer was to the all-too obvious question of whether I thought IPSO was a success. It was almost impossible to resist answering with the Professor Joad-like response (when will the BBC bring back *The Brains Trust*?): "it all depends what you mean by success". Success to the reader meant a front-page splash signed by the editor and confessing to guilt. To the newspaper, it meant the evidence of the used bank-notes in a brown paper bag, but to the disinterested observer...?

The Importance of Self-Interest

Let me make the more limited assertion that no system of regulation will work unless the regulated believe that it is in their own interest to be regulated. Such an assertion is easier to demonstrate in the case of the professions: you can create and maintain a cadre of respected and financially rewarding expertise, if entry to the profession is difficult, and if breaches of the rules of conduct may lead to ignominy and expulsion. Many industries, too, saw that it was in their own interest, for their own protection, that regulations were in place to safeguard the public: the nuclear and pharmaceutical industries are obvious examples.

But there are other more subtle, or, let it be admitted, more insidious reasons why self-interest is important to regulation, whether the system of regulation is underpinned by statute, contract, or is even purely voluntary (like the former systems of press regulation in the UK). Unless there is a willing acceptance of the authority of the regulator, there is a natural tendency towards resistance and secrecy. The regulated find it all too easy to be obstructive and obscurantist; it is inevitable that when rules are drafted they will fail to foresee and therefore fail to cover situations arising in the future. Indeed, rules should not be too precise for fear they will become too rigid and inflexible within the strait-jacket of precise definitions. They become fertile battle-grounds for disputes as to interpretation and application. Investigations lead to secrecy and, sometimes, concealment and destruction of evidence. A miasma of resentment wafts over the disputes. These elements of the relationship between the regulated and their regulator exist whether the regulation is imposed by Parliament under statute or by the will of the regulated.

Taming the BBC?

What then of the BBC and *Ofcom*? How often I have envied the fact that public service broadcasting was not only controlled under a system of statutory licensing but that the rules themselves contained highfalutin concepts, so strange to the world of the press, of, for example, 'fairness' and 'taste'. I grew to understand at IPSO that the worst aspects of the press were often those which were the least susceptible to control and regulation. How do you regulate against cruelty, bullying and offensiveness particularly when directed against those who find it almost impossible to protect themselves? Yet these were features that individuals and the public as a whole most disliked and feared.

Each generation of reader lacks historical perspective. It believes that media behaviour is deteriorating. That is not true. The hounding by the Northcliffe press of Lord Haldane is an early 20th Century reminder of what was rumoured to be the then Lord Rothermere's answer to the question as to why his newspapers were so successful: *I give the people someone to hate every day*. No-one has yet come up with an answer as to how regulation might control press cruelty or bullying.

And yet and yet. Of course they have. Why cannot we emulate *Ofcom*? Why cannot we be all like the BBC or other Public Broadcasters, controlled by licence and required to avoid anything which might be thought tasteless and offensive? (Unless you are too *Guardian*-like to require control and your piety makes even an angel's wing droop). The question need only to be asked for the answer to become apparent. Balance leads all too soon to lack of controversy and lack of controversy to a world of master-cooking and mistress-dancing; there is often a feeble imprecision in the BBC's ability to hold politicians to account, an absence of stringency and gravity. The public broadcaster's belief that balance means equal air-time, coupled with the fear that the governmental purse-keeper will starve them into submission leads to a grey and damp cloud hanging over the broadcaster. It is no accident that managers proliferate in inverse proportion to newsgatherers and reporters. Fear drives them to kow-tow. There is, I suggest, far too much time given to allow those answerable to the public to refuse to answer. And it is, to a major degree, the result of the content and application of the rules, imposed by statute and now administered by *Ofcom* which leads to the bland leading the bland.

Who needs regulation anyway?

Perhaps my envy of a statutory regulator is misplaced. My aspirations would be better focussed on my belief that we might do better with no regulation at all. The newspaper proprietor's credo that he is giving the public what it wants carries with it the danger and the sanction that a newspaper must be fearful of offending its adherent reader. *The Sun* was forced to dismiss its' former editor when he spewed a thoughtless insult about a popular footballer; no newspaper dares to be offensive about the Queen or Prince Philip. This is not the result of regulation but because the readers would not buy either the insults or the newspaper.

What is required is to induce into the few who read newspapers a sense of empowerment, the notion that they can take control, that the newspaper proprietor is not as powerful as he thinks he is. I believe that there is a solution.

It would be worth trying a period without regulation; no regulation for anyone, neither broadcasters, nor the press. I doubt whether they would behave worse, they are far too conscious of the need to attract readers, listeners and viewers. Of course, they might resort to more all-baking, sous-vide excursions into *vox pop* but even they might weary of their tendency to safety. Would it not be worth a try for a limited period? The depressing feature which both legislation and regulation share is the inability to change direction. Too often, once brought into force, laws or regulations are never abolished or once abolished are never revived. But what is wrong with a trial? We need to introduce the notion of experiment into regulation and legislation. The leviathan of *Ofcom* might welcome a release of its ponderous duties for a period and do we really believe that will change the behaviour of the BBC, make it better or worse? It is a realistic possibility that it will become less flabby, and adopt a more Robinson-like approach to cross-examination of our leaders. (Do not think I am being over-critical, the feebleness of the totality of broadcasters and press in their cross-examination of Dominic Cummings was almost unwatchable).

So too in the case of newspapers, I believe we would be no worse off and might receive greater advantage from a period without regulation at all. So here, late in the day as it is, is my application (C.V and references to follow): to become chair of *Ofcom* and then remove from its responsibility the regulation of all public service broadcasting.

I don't think I'll get the job.

About the Contributor

Alan Moses served as a barrister, High Court Judge, and Lord Justice in the Court of Appeal before leaving to become the first Chairman of IPSO, the Press Regulator. He was educated at Bryanston and University College Oxford. Formerly Chairman of Spitalfields Music, he is now a Court of Appeal Justice of the Cayman Islands, but is otherwise looking for offers.

Chapter Two

Can *Ofcom* pull off the political/technocratic confidence trick?

> Bill Emmott, the former Editor in Chief of *The Economist*, was inside the belly of the *Ofcom* beast, but then he was out! He reflects on whether the regulator can ride two horses at the same time...

If it works for central banks or railway regulators, why shouldn't it work for communications, whether the telecom form or the televisual? In my view, that was the spirit in which the Office for Communications, *Ofcom*, was brought into being nearly two decades ago as the latest example of a kind of political confidence-trick: that by handing the power, and even more the responsibility, over awkward, often controversial issues to a body of unelected experts such issues could be handled in a quieter, more technical way, ideally a way that incorporates long-term thinking rather than tomorrow's headlines. To call it a political confidence-trick is not to say it was wrong or unreasonable, as the example of the Bank of England since it was made independent in 1997 shows. Getting the Bank an arm or two's length away from the hothouses of Parliament and Whitehall has made monetary policy steadier, more transparent and somewhat more predictable.

Ofcom pulls off the trick? Tame the BBC tiger?

For much of the time, the trick has worked with *Ofcom* too, just as it has with other regulatory "Offices" such as Ofwat, Ofgem and Ofrail. The trouble is, it has worked too well for *Ofcom's* own good, and the agency also happens to be presiding over one of the – perhaps *the* – most rapidly changing and expanding industries in the world.

Ofcom's technocratic competence, combined with the complexity and salience of the whole digital revolution, have encouraged successive governments to load more and more responsibilities on to its unelected, technocrat shoulders. But there is only so much that technocratic shoulders can really bear. There is a limit to how far politically sensitive issues can really be de-politicised by putting them in the hands of experts. There is a limit to how far public confidence in this political con-trick can be maintained.

When the government decided in March 2016 to hand over regulation of the BBC (Public Service) to *Ofcom* with full effect from the beginning of the new Royal Charter in 2017, the limit was breached. The political elastic, to change metaphors, had been stretched too far. It has snapped.

The idea of transferring responsibility for regulating the BBC to *Ofcom* was perfectly logical when it came to the fore in 2015. The real question is whether it was practical. It was logical because *Ofcom* already had the responsibility of managing the licensing of all other broadcasters on both television and radio in the United Kingdom. And it already had the responsibility of enforcing the provisions of the Broadcasting Code for all those broadcasters and, indirectly, for the BBC too.

Viewers' complaints about BBC output were going in the first instance to the BBC itself and then to the BBC Trust (as to the previous governance body, the BBC Governors), and could in principle be appealed to *Ofcom*. The agency therefore already had expertise about licensing, the Broadcasting Code and complaints. With the BBC Governors and then the BBC Trust having fallen out of political favour having been perceived to have been discredited by their failure to deal effectively with successive scandals at the Corporation, why not resort to the usual confidence trick of handing regulation of the UK's one global media giant, the BBC, over to the clever technocrats at *Ofcom*?

On paper, it made perfect sense.

But in practice?

Now take the logic to its, well, logical conclusion, as may well soon be on the cards for *Ofcom*. If it makes sense to place all broadcasting, public or private, under this one, technocratic, arms'-length agency, it presumably makes sense to give *Ofcom* oversight of all the main platforms through which video and audio news and comment are distributed and viewed, in other words the digital platforms of *Twitter, YouTube, Facebook, Google, Apple, Amazon* and any others that may hove into view in the future. After all, why should it make sense to impose the broadcasting code's requirements – and, recently, punish them through fines and licence withdrawals – on state-run TV entities such as *Russia Today (RT), China Global Television Network(CGTN)* or Iran's *Press TV*, but not on equally propagandising outlets that choose to disseminate their versions of the news to the British public through social media on digital platforms rather than through old-fashioned satellite television?

Plainly, it doesn't: either the "due impartiality" requirement of the Broadcasting Code should be imposed on all, or on none; or conceivably some sort of threshold of audience reach could be used to distinguish between those worthy of *Ofcom's* steely, technocratic graze and those who can be disregarded. The already mighty *Ofcom* should, will, must, be given further powers and responsibilities simply reflecting the nature, power and importance of the digital revolution through which we are all living. We live not just in the information age but the disinformation age: who better to deal with that than *Ofcom*?

That is absolutely where the logic of the BBC decision leads, and is, really, the logic of *Ofcom's* remit. But the question is whether it would be possible, for such a mighty and comprehensive body to make the political confidence-trick of technocratic regulation work. The experience of 2015-17 and the transfer of the BBC tells me that it cannot, at least not without a substantial rethink of *Ofcom's* structure, accountability and transparency.

Brexit and broadcasting

Perhaps the timing was unlucky: the fact that the transfer of regulatory responsibility over the BBC to *Ofcom* coincided with the most divisive political issue for decades, namely Brexit. And it was: there could be no gradual easing into the role, no smooth transition, when for all broadcasters the issue of "due impartiality" over Brexit had become the hottest political potato of all. Yet actually, the timing would always have been unlucky, whenever the transfer had taken place. For the fundamental problem would have raised its head eventually, over one issue or another: can a technocratic, arm's length regulatory agency such as *Ofcom* really mediate disputes surrounding public broadcasting and impartiality which are unavoidably political and carry with them the fates of political parties and individual politicians?

Ofcom and I: a marriage not made in heaven

This inconvenient truth became evident as soon as the Brexit Referendum took place on June 23 2016, which was even before *Ofcom* had formally taken over supervision of the BBC. It became evident through the medium of one individual, a man who had been appointed to the board of *Ofcom* only in January of that year.

Yes, that man was yours truly.

My experience with *Ofcom* and with its ministerial overseer, the Department for Culture, Media and Sport, is mainly – of course – of interest to me. But although my particular fate is not of wider significance, I offer it here as a case study of what an impossible position *Ofcom* was really in once it had been decided that its reach should be expanded to take in the BBC. And, although it seems funny only in retrospect, what became sort-of amusing but also puzzling was how little the senior executives at *Ofcom* had understood about what sort of impossible position they were getting themselves into.

Here's my story.

During 2015, the *Ofcom* chair, Dame Patricia Hodgson, and by extension the chief executive, Sharon White (now Dame Sharon), played the perfect part of generals fighting the last war. The reason why the BBC Governors and the BBC Trust were seen as discredited, they believed, was that they were perceived as being too close to the BBC itself. They had become cheerleaders or defenders of the Beeb, so how could they be credible regulators?

If *Ofcom* was to be credible as a better regulator, it had to show that it was not overly close to the BBC, that it was not going to be just another cheerleader. Given that Dame Patricia herself had enjoyed a long and distinguished career at the BBC, including as The Secretary and as Director of Policy and Planning, culminating in membership of the BBC Trust, she was naturally very conscious of this issue.

A vacancy on the *Ofcom* board had come up thanks to the fact that Tim Gardam, by then Principal of St Anne's College Oxford but previously a highly regarded producer at the BBC (and former Director of Television at Channel Four), had come to the end of his term. His board seat came with another responsibility: chairmanship of *Ofcom's* Content Board, a board of about 20 people with no fiduciary responsibility but charged with advising the main board on all matters to do with broadcasting standards and quality, including enforcement of the code. In seeking a replacement for Gardam, it was decided that a change was needed: rather than recruiting another broadcaster with, inevitably, past ties to the BBC, the board would seek someone with high-level editorial experience elsewhere in the media. That way, *Ofcom* could be seen to be truly independent from the BBC.

Bring in Emmott..

That's what led to me, a former editor-in-chief of *The Economist,* being solicited by *Ofcom*'s head-hunter to apply and then to my being recommended by the recruitment panel and appointed formally in December 2015 by the then Secretary of State at the DCMS, John Whittingdale. Although no longer at *The Economist,* I was still writing, though mainly for Italian and Japanese publications and for Project Syndicate, and had executive produced a documentary about the EU that was shown on BBC Four that same year, *The Great European Disaster Movie.* This was all disclosed and discussed, and it was agreed that I could continue with the type and limited extent of journalism I was already doing. The sole condition applied, and perfectly reasonably, was that I must not take an active role in any political campaigns, including over the forthcoming Brexit Referendum.

All was fine, until the Referendum was approaching and the political temperature was getting hotter. I wasn't campaigning, but occasionally my writing for those non-British outlets had to mention the main UK event under way, namely the Referendum. The *Ofcom* executive started to get cold feet about me being on the board, and especially chairing the Content Board. The Referendum happened, went the way it did, and soon afterwards word spread that the new Secretary of State, Karen Bradley, was getting pressure from Conservative MPs about *Ofcom* and the suitability of having a known Remainer chairing the Content Board.

Whether or not that pressure was, in the end, the reason, both Hodgson and White decided I had to go. One could argue, and they doubtless will, that while still not being either a political campaigner or an active commentator in the UK media I had not been silent enough.

This isn't the place to argue the toss about that. We negotiated a more-or-less amicable settlement of my departure, which the *Ofcom* Company Secretary said just needed approval by the Secretary of

State, which should come in a few days. It didn't. Finally, about four months later, Karen Bradley made her decision: rather than being given any sort of settlement for the abrupt termination of my contract, I was instead to be dismissed for "gross misconduct".

To cut this long story short, I'm afraid I refused to be a good chap and resign just ahead of the termination, which the DCMS Permanent Secretary, Sue Owen, advised me to do. I took out a case for judicial review of the Secretary of State's decision, and, after a lot of aggravation and expense, Bradley's successor in that role, one Matt Hancock, eventually instructed his officials and lawyers to settle the case and agree to a statement withdrawing the accusation of misconduct.

Lessons from my *Ofcom* nightmare

Enough of my axe-grinding, you may well say. What are the wider lessons of this episode? They are, first, simply that the well-meaning *Ofcom* executive blundered in its thinking about the appointment to replace Gardam, and then got caught in the political headlights. Second, *Ofcom* is supposed to be politically independent, but evidently had their own definition as to what this might mean. As I am afraid I felt bound at the time to point out, among its then just six non-executive directors there were three with close ties to the Conservative Party – Hodgson, an intimate of Margaret Thatcher and former chair of the Bow Group; Sheila Noakes, a Tory peer; and Graham Mather, a former Tory MEP. Thus the fact that half the board had connections, in one case highly active, with one political party was evidently deemed less salient than the fact that the chair of the Content Board -me- was a known Remainer. It is all about public *perceptions* of bias, I was told, which made one wonder why the public would feel concerned about a Content Board in which one opinion among 20 went a particular way on Brexit, but not about a board of directors in which 50% had Tory connections.

Third, that *Ofcom's* internal codes of conduct, designed to guide my conduct as well as all other board members, are deliberately ambiguous, such that my own actions, which had anyway been cleared with the appointment panel, could be interpreted both as permitted and not permitted. (I could explain, but you'd find it too tedious.) But mainly, fourth, that in the face of political attack or controversy, *Ofcom* really feels it has no choice but to hunker down and try to keep as low a profile as possible. White's view, as expressed to me, was not unreasonable in the circumstances: that for *Ofcom* there is no upside to profile or public scrutiny, only potential downside.

As the Irish song goes, 'whatever you say, say nothing...'

To repeat, so as to underline: this is not unreasonable. However, while this approach may well be suitable for overseeing the allocation of spectrum, or other technical telecoms matters, can it really be sustained by the principal overseer of the BBC, let alone one which may in future quite logically become overseer of news output on digital platforms too? Without some sort of really robust public status, guaranteeing its independence while maintaining political credibility and ultimate accountability, it is already hard to see *Ofcom* being able to be the solution to the long-running BBC problem: how to regulate the public broadcasting behemoth without becoming its cheerleader or its sap, and how to do so without being perceived as party political.

Since 2017, it has therefore chosen to keep its oversight of the BBC as quiet as a mouse. How this approach will survive whatever is the next scandal remains to be seen.

Has the confidence trick failed?

It is not impossible that the political confidence-trick of technocratic independence could be pulled off for communications, with sufficient change to *Ofcom*'s status and structure. It needs a robust public presence and voice, and credibility both about its competence and its independence.

I would argue that the Bank of England isn't a bad model: the Monetary Policy Committee of the Bank includes four outsiders among its nine members. They are appointed by the Chancellor of the Exchequer, just as appointments to *Ofcom*'s board are formally made by the Secretary of State of the DCMS. But unlike at *Ofcom*, the external members are not barred from having or publishing professional opinions (almost all have been economists) but are simply barred from public comment about imminent MPC decisions. Their known possession of professional opinions forms part of their, and the MPC's, credibility.

However, in addition to going for MPC-style externals you'd probably have to establish the CEO or Chair of *Ofcom* as a person of independent standing, expertise and voice, analogous to that of the Governor of the Bank of England, who would then manage a body of technocrats to do the detailed work but chair decision-making boards in which no individual could be seen to be dominant. This still would leave *Ofcom* stretched hugely wide and it is genuinely hard to imagine who might be the communications equivalents of Andrew Bailey or Mark Carney. But what is clear is that the current pretence is unsustainable.

About the Contributor

Bill Emmott is a writer best known for his 13 years as Editor of *The Economist* (1993-2006), a publication he joined in 1980 and served in London, Brussels and Tokyo. He is currently chair of the International Institute for Strategic Studies, of the Japan Society of the UK, and of Trinity College Dublin's research institute for arts & humanities. He has co-written or executive-produced two documentaries shown on BBC Four: *Girlfriend in a Coma* (2013), and *The Great European Disaster Movie* (2015).

Chapter Three

Has *Ofcom* forgotten its roots?

> *Ofcom*'s duty to further the interests of citizens, which emerged after a long political struggle, has been vital to its central role in promoting the democratic and cultural benefits of broadcasting. Recent evidence suggests that *Ofcom* may be losing its focus on citizens. Professor Steven Barnett.

It was not an easy birth. Almost exactly 20 years ago, in October 2001, the paving bill to set up a shadow *Ofcom* was sent to the House of Lords. Tensions that had simmered for years had broken out into open warfare between those who favoured a hands-off economic approach (as preferred by the old Department for Trade and Industry) and the pro public service interventionists of DCMS. Plans for the converged regulator were confused and, in terms of the guiding principles still being debated, distinctly unconverged. I wrote of a still embryonic *Ofcom* in the Observer: "At the heart of the *Ofcom* issue lies a fundamental dilemma: an unresolved philosophical chasm in the Government's White Paper between its economic mission and its cultural mission. On the one hand, it wants to 'make the UK home to the most dynamic and competitive communications and media market in the world'. On the other, it wants to 'make sure that our citizens can continue to rely on, and enjoy, public service broadcasting which is widely admired and envied'."[1]

Triumph of the citizens' interests

There followed throughout 2002-3 an almighty battle by the DCMS vanguard – alongside civil society groups, academics and a platoon of sympathetic politicians – to ensure that the final incarnation would explicitly embrace DCMS priorities through the shorthand of a commitment to "citizens". Old hands will remember well a Downing Street insistence that "citizens" had a narrow legalistic meaning attached to immigration status and nationality, which could not

---

[1] *Observer*, 14 October 2001:
https://www.theguardian.com/media/2001/oct/14/ofcom.broadcasting.

possibly be absorbed into general legislation on the future of communications.

And so, in its first iteration emerging from the DTI in December 2000, the Communications White Paper referenced both consumers and citizens. Eighteen months later, however, the draft Bill had dropped any reference to citizens and gave *Ofcom* the duty only to further the interests of broadcasting and telecoms customers. This was firmly rejected by the cross-party pre-legislative scrutiny committee chaired by Lord Puttnam, which recommended that *Ofcom* should have two principal duties: to further the interests of both citizens and of consumers. Despite the clear objection from all parties represented on the Puttnam committee, the next iteration of the Communications Bill in November 2002 specified only that *Ofcom* was "to further the interests of consumers in relevant markets, where appropriate by promoting competition". Once again, Downing Street was insisting that an explicit commitment to citizens was unnecessary.

Despite the then Labour government's 167 Commons majority, it faced a backlash in the House of Lords. In a Lords second reading debate on 25 March, Lord McNally articulated the discomfort felt across all parties: "The charge against Ministers and against this Bill from these Benches is that, unamended, the Bill puts too much faith in the whimsical destructiveness of the market and pays too little attention to the protection of the interests of the citizen and the wider cultural and democratic responsibilities of the industries involved."[1]

At the final Report stage in the Lords, in June 2003, the government failed in a last ditch attempt to resist the Puttnam amendment and lost by a decisive 179 votes to 75.[2] As a result, Clause 3(1)of the Communications Act passed the following month stipulates that:

'It shall be the principal duty of *Ofcom*, in carrying out their functions; (a) to further the interests of citizens in relation to communications matters; and (b) to further the interests of consumers in relevant markets, where appropriate by promoting competition'.

---

[1] Hansard: https://api.parliament.uk/historic-hansard/lords/2003/mar/25/communications-bill, Col 669.

[2] Hansard: https://api.parliament.uk/historic-hansard/lords/2003/jun/23/communications-bill, Col 11.

Why the duty to citizens matters

Whatever the reasons for the Blair policy unit's insistence that this was not an important distinction, it was sophistry: the distinction mattered then and it matters even more now. In a speech to the Westminster Media Forum shortly after the Act was passed, Ed Richards – the main architect of *Ofcom* from within Downing Street and subsequently its CEO – outlined some crucial areas of difference between citizenship and consumerism. These included long term vs short term focus; private benefit vs public or social benefit; language of choice vs language of rights; and regulation *against* detriment vs regulation *for* the public interest.[1] The philosopher Lady Onora O'Neill, who contributed to the Lords debate, drew her own distinction the previous year in her Reith lectures on Trust: "Citizens, it is said, no longer trust governments, or politicians, or ministers, or the police, or the courts, or the prison service. Consumers, it is said, no longer trust business, especially big business, or their products".[2]

Citizenship, in other words, extends far beyond consumption. At its broadest level, it is about the sort of society – or sort of country – we want to live in even if that conflicts with or inhibits our consumption choices. We like driving, but we accept that road safety – and climate change – demands some restrictions; we don't have children, but accept that a well educated society obliges us to contribute to schools; we haven't been a victim of crime, but want a criminal justice system that penalises wrongdoing and keeps us safe; we contribute to – and appreciate the existence of – well-maintained public spaces, cleaner air, museums and art galleries even when we don't "consume" them.

These citizenship attributes apply equally to our communicative space. We accept that an element of our licence fee should fund *Radio 3* or *CBeebies* even if we hate classical music and our children are in their twenties. We enjoy the connectedness and liberating ease of social media, but want action to prevent the bullying, abuse, grooming and racism which seem to have proliferated – and we look with trepidation

---

[1] Quoted in Sonia Livingstone, "What is the citizen's interest in communication regulation? Ofcom's agenda for 'Citizens, communications and convergence'", paper presented to the Media, Communication and Humanity Conference, 2008: http://eprints.lse.ac.uk/21561/1/whatisthecitizeninterestin(LSEROversion).pdf.

[2] Onora O'Neill, *A Question of Trust*, 2002: https://www.bbc.co.uk/radio4/reith2002/lecture1.shtml.

across the Atlantic at how online platforms have been exploited to radicalise vulnerable and isolated citizens.

As democrats, we want to encourage a plurality of news sources from all over the world, but we are aware that information can be distorted by malign actors and we seek reassurance that robust and effective regulatory structures are in place to foster accurate journalism, expose disinformation and inhibit its dissemination. It is not a coincidence that trust in broadcast journalism remains high, while the UK consistently languishes at the bottom of European trust tables for print media:[1] while impartiality rules and codes of journalistic conduct have long been independently monitored and implemented by *Ofcom* (and its regulatory predecessors), the press has seen decades of weak and ineffectual oversight of its journalistic codes by industry-dominated regulators (of which *IPSO* is the latest).[2]

Of course, the "we" is not one of unanimous consent. There are free-wheeling libertarians who still object to compulsory seat-belts in cars (not to mention enforced lockdowns during a pandemic), additional taxes on diesel fuel, any element of the BBC licence fee, and any constraint on publishing material, however hateful, harmful, inaccurate or dangerous to democracy. But as the general acceptance of lockdown rules proved (aside from occasional trips to Barnard Castle and a few poorly attended demonstrations), most are prepared to forego some individual gratification to further the collective good.

But *Ofcom* is losing its citizen focus…

To what extent *Ofcom* is still immersed in that culture is a matter of concern, particularly since adopting the regulatory mantle of the BBC. On one reading, taking on responsibility for an institution whose very existence has been defined as a contribution to British cultural, democratic and economic welfare should sit perfectly with its citizenship duty. But when this transfer of power was being debated, I

---

[1] In the most recent EBU research, 75% in the UK said that they "tend not to trust" the written press. This was by far the biggest trust gap of all 33 nations included in the survey: *Trust in Media 2020*, EBU, June 2020, p32.

[2] I have written in more detail about the recurring pattern of industry-compromised press regulation for Democratic Audit, 21 May 2018:
https://www.democraticaudit.com/2018/05/21/the-government-scuppers-leveson-part-2-is-britains-press-undermining-democracy/.

and many others were nervous that it could have the opposite effect: that the competition and consumerist side of *Ofcom's* corporate psyche would be leveraged to the BBC's disadvantage.

Signs so far are not encouraging.

First, there was the long delay in allowing the BBC more flexibility in its iPlayer, to enable it to compete with increasing audience demand for box sets and longer viewing windows. *Ofcom's* insistence on launching a Public Interest Test after the BBC's Unitary Board had announced its decision was not the approach of a regulator that was prioritising the interests of citizens who were collectively paying for a universal public service competing with American streaming services. Nor was it helpful that the process, from *Ofcom's* intervention in November 2018 until its final determination in August 2019, took 9 months in a world of rapidly changing audience consumption habits. In the words of then BBC chairman Sir David Clementi, it was an approach that ran the risk of "tying ourselves up in red tape and regulation at a time when media organisations need to be fast and agile".[1]

Then there was the strange case of the BBC and impartiality. *Ofcom's* 2020 News Consumption report gave figures for how audiences rated seven TV providers on nine separate news attributes, including impartiality.[2] But these figures were calculated only on the basis of "regular users" of each service, which distorted the data: on every single attribute CNN (222 regular viewers in the *Ofcom* sample) emerged as top. On impartiality, Al Jazeera (153 regular viewers) was second only to CNN, with 69%. The equivalent BBC figure was 58% but on a sample size of 2,754 because BBC news is the default choice for most TV viewers and commands huge audiences. At the very least, such figures have to be treated with caution because we can be pretty sure that regular viewers of, say, Fox News would rate it very highly for impartiality.

---

[1] Speech to the Oxford Media Convention, 18 March 2019:
https://www.bbc.co.uk/mediacentre/speeches/2019/clementi-omc.

[2] Ofcom, *News Consumption in the UK: 2020* Figure 11.5, p73,
https://www.ofcom.org.uk/__data/assets/pdf_file/0013/201316/news-consumption-2020-report.pdf.

How was this questionable data reported in *Ofcom's* annual report on the BBC? In a two-page section under the tendentious heading *"Audiences continue to rate the* BBC *lower on impartiality"*, *Ofcom* recognised that the BBC faces greater scrutiny than other news organisations but did not acknowledge either the huge political (and rival media) attacks on BBC impartiality nor the vast differences in base sizes for their data.[1] Unsurprisingly, no mention was made of either CNN or Al Jazeera, which would immediately have raised questions about their interpretation of the data.

Equally unsurprisingly – and *Ofcom* would have anticipated this – its headlined conclusion featured prominently in negative coverage by a highly partisan press. A rather more nuanced – and citizen-based – approach might have reported on a 2020 Ipsos-Mori study with fieldwork at roughly the same time. When a representative sample of *all adults* was asked "Which one source are you most likely to turn to if you want impartial news coverage", 51% responded BBC. The next highest, with just 7%, was Sky News.[2]

Finally, we have *Ofcom*'s consultation on the future of public service broadcasting, published in December 2020.[3] In attempting, quite properly, to address how a revised regulatory framework for PSB might embrace new technologies such as smart TVs, subscription platforms, and voice-activated delivery, it proposed shifting from the concept of Public Service Broadcasting to Public Service Media. This reframing raised awkward questions about whether *Ofcom* continued to believe in an institution-based approach. For while the consultation document talked about a "PSM framework" and a "PSM system" - both of which might be centred around institutional providers – it also referred to "how PSM is made" and "PSM content".

Such a redefinition inevitably places undue emphasis on consumerist, market-gap arguments favoured by those who have long believed that

---

[1] Ofcom, *Ofcom's annual report on the BBC* 2019/20, pp31-3,
https://www.ofcom.org.uk/__data/assets/pdf_file/0021/207228/third-bbc-annual-report.pdf.

[2] https://www.ipsos.com/sites/default/files/ct/news/documents/2020-05/trust-accuracy-impartiality-2020.pdf, p6.

[3] Ofcom, Small Screen: Big Debate Consultation, 8 December 2020:
https://www.smallscreenbigdebate.co.uk/__data/assets/pdf_file/0032/208769/consultation-future-of-public-service-media.pdf.

broadcasting should be left to the market-place. PSB is founded on citizen-based values of range, quality, universality, impartiality, innovation, and wide geographic appeal that are rooted in institutions, not content. It is not at all clear that *Ofcom* today understands or accepts that distinction.

Resisting the political mood

These may be straws in the wind, but they are blowing in one direction only. Since its inauguration in 2003, *Ofcom* has played a critical role in promoting the UK's democratic and cultural welfare. It was an almighty battle to have the citizens' interests included in its core responsibilities, and over the years that obligation has defined its approach to PSB, and to impartiality and accuracy. There are now disturbing signs that its decision-making and internal culture is increasingly dominated by an economistic and consumerist philosophy which is at odds with its duty to citizens.

This is no doubt in part a silent acknowledgement (which *Ofcom* would vigorously deny) of a toxic political environment which is dominated by a right-wing Conservative government that has made little secret of its desire to insinuate its ideology into every aspect of British public life. In particular, since taking over regulatory oversight of the BBC in 2017, it is unclear to what extent *Ofcom* values an institution that represents a deliberate and distorting intervention in the market-place to further the interests of citizens. If that parliamentary battle spearheaded by Lord Puttnam 18 years ago is not to be in vain, a campaign may be needed to save *Ofcom* from the ravages of today's culture wars and remind it of its statutory duty to citizens.

About the Contributor

Steven Barnett is Professor of Communications at the University of Westminster and an established writer, author and commentator, who specialises in communications policy and regulation. Over the last 35 years, he has advised ministers and shadow ministers across the political spectrum, has given evidence to Parliamentary committees and has served several times as specialist adviser to the House of Lords Communications and Digital Committee. He is on the editorial and management boards of the *British Journalism Review*, and was for many years an *Observer* columnist. *Books include The Rise and Fall of*

Television Journalism (Bloomsbury, 2011) and *Media Power and Plurality (with Judith Townend, eds*, Palgrave, 2015).

Chapter Four

The Lie in the Machine: Big tech and the limits of free speech

Much of the regulatory time for *Ofcom* in the future may be taken up by trying to ride the tiger of the US tech giants-the so called FAANGS. Former BBC Director General and New York Times CEO Mark Thompson draws lessons from 'over there' for 'over here'.

Former President Trump and a number of congressional Republicans have talked up the possibility of removing the extensive immunity digital companies enjoy from legal action over the content they distribute unless those companies *also* agree to give equal prominence to rightwing voices. This seems to constitute a proposal to compel speech and would probably founder in the courts in the unlikely event it made it into law.

In the UK, the Secretary of State for Education has announced the creation of a "free speech Champion" for English universities – instantly of course dubbed a free speech Tsar – and promised "strong, robust action" if undertakings on freedom of expression are breached. But enforcing free speech is a ludicrous contradiction in terms and the invention of a free speech champion or tsar or commissar one that George Orwell himself would have been proud of.

I believe that students *should* have the chance to encounter a wide range of different perspectives and that, while they have every right to protest at an invitation to someone whose views they find hateful or unacceptable, other students or the universities themselves have the right to ignore those protests. But universities are independent institutions full of free citizens – they shouldn't be compelled to invite or disinvite anyone. The Secretary of State frets about the "chilling effect" of "woke culture", but there's nothing more chilling in the realm of freedom of expression than "strong, robust action" by governments.

Must you carry?

There is no principle of "must carry" within the broader right to free expression, no right to be invited to give a talk or to have your views published or distributed by anyone. If you don't like what the papers are saying about you, you should do what that great American founding father Alexander Hamilton did and start your own. If you think all the existing universities are too "woke", found one where everyone can get a good night's sleep.

Donald Trump may well have been within his First Amendment rights when he recklessly whipped up his supporters on January 6 2021 (before they thrashed the Capitol). But the major digital platforms are *certainly* within their constitutional rights to decide that his messages were dangerous and dishonest and to ban him for life if they chose to.

And, to state the obvious, no platform or publication has any legal or moral obligation to disseminate hateful lies like the ones contained in QAnon – indeed it's deeply regrettable that the major platforms waited so long to begin the arduous work of rooting it out. It's probably impossible to expunge the racist conspiracy theories completely but pushing them out of the sunlight and into the shadowy margins of digital space is still eminently worthwhile.

Banning Trump from Twitter...

What should we make of (founder) Jack Dorsey's thoughtful remark that his own decision to ban Donald Trump from Twitter was a "bad precedent"? I don't believe it was in terms of freedom of expression. But there's another consideration – which is about the extraordinary concentration of power that lies in his hands and those of a handful of other leaders in tech.

Because one can believe that the major platforms behaved responsibly in this instance and still worry about what would happen if one of them had taken the opposite view, or ejected a president or political party for purely personal reasons, or indeed fallen themselves under the spell of QAnon.

Is Digital power in too few hands?

Is it really acceptable that half a dozen companies – perhaps in the end half a dozen individuals – should wield so much influence over, if not the totality of content available on the internet, then that portion which most people consume most of the time? What protections are there against the purely arbitrary exercise of this great power?

The winner-take-most character of algorithmic digital services – and the amazing success a handful of companies have had in engaging and monetizing vast audiences poses questions about competitions and markets that regulators are now taking seriously in many jurisdictions. But the same mass engagement has also had the effect of concentrating power over content distribution.

Regulating first broadcasting and now the internet?

In the 20th century policymakers confronted exactly this problem in broadcasting. Spectrum was scarce and the radio stations and TV channels necessarily few and so disproportionately influential. As a result, governments everywhere – even the United States – put in regimes of content regulation that would have been unthinkable for newspapers and magazines.

One can sense many politicians on both sides of the Atlantic itching to do something similar in the case of the major digital platforms.

I'm against it – or at least against it unless it turns out to be the only workable solution. Governments themselves have enormous conflicts of interest when it comes to content regulation, and even if you happen to trust the government in power in your country, what guarantee do you have that the next one will be able to resist using the levers of regulation to suit itself?

Is peer review a better way?

The history of media suggests that professional peer review, input from civil society and reputational pressure do a far better job of guiding the establishment of sophisticated editorial standards – for instance what do you decide *not* to print because, though not illegal, it may be offensive or hurtful to some – than law or regulation. Tastes change, old concerns recede and new ones arise, and a plural marketplace of standards and standard-setters can flex and evolve with them. The standards are collective judgements and necessarily provisional. A brave editor may choose to challenge them – though she or he may have to take on some professional risk if they do – but this constant arguing and testing of the boundaries is itself a way of ensuring relevance and responsiveness over time.

Is Facebook showing us the way to self-regulation?

Even a disaggregated and informal system of standards requires ways of dealing with complaints and appeals – which is why Facebook's Oversight Board is so interesting. This is a group of external experts who've been chosen by Facebook to review its decisions and whose judgements the company says it will abide by. The board has already reversed four *Facebook* judgement calls and they'll soon be opining on that Trump ban – their appeal for public submissions on that case has just closed.

Now it's not perfect. The members of the board look very credible to me, but they were chosen by Facebook and the call by one of them, Alan Rusbridger (the former *Guardian* editor), for proper access to the algorithm which makes most of Facebook's content judgement calls, suggests they don't yet feel they have all the information they need to do their job properly.

Better if it were fully independent and the members independently selected. Better if there were more than one such board and if some of the boards adjudicated for more than one company. Better if the transparency about how the major platform's algorithms work was extended not just to the great and good around the oversight board table but to every user. And so on. But for all that, the board seems to me to be a significant step in the right direction.

I hope the other big players watch it closely.

The internet – heaven or hell?

The internet left the Garden of Eden a long time ago now. The web magnifies and accelerates everything, the bad as well as the good, and it turns out not just that human nature doesn't change as rapidly as technology, but that it doesn't change much at all.

QAnon and other similar dark products of the human id adapt and mutate and ebb and flow, but they don't go away. Like background viruses, we're probably going to be living with them forever.

But no publisher or platform on earth has any legal or moral obligation to spread them or indeed to distribute any form of prejudice or hate. So, eject them from your platform if you can, and ban their authors for life.

There will be hard cases – for instance when racist conspiracies get tangled up with electoral politics and the lines are hard to draw – but, at least to me, January 2021 and the Capitol proved that not just venerable news organisations but relatively young digital companies can figure their way through them.

But those digital companies will only remain free from regulatory control if they move quickly to establish secure checks and balances to ensure that the unprecedented power they have over what the world sees and hears cannot be abused.

All of this is urgent. The world moves a lot faster now than it did in 13th Century England. Then, Little St Hugh was murdered as a result of a false 'blood libel' – an anti-Jewish witch hunt in 1255. This time, we won't get seven hundred years to put up a plaque to say we're sorry we got it wrong.

We may not even get seven.

This is an edited version of the Philip Geddes Memorial Lecture delivered by Mark Thompson 'in' Oxford on March 5th 2021. Reproduced with the author's permission.

About the Contributor

Mark Thompson is the former CEO and President of the New York Times, Director General of the BBC, and CEO of Channel Four Television.

Chapter Five

Over here, over there: Why the US News Jungle shows just why we need broadcast regulation in the UK

Clive Myrie -2021 Royal Television Society Journalist of the year and 2021 RTS Network News Presenter of the year looks across the Atlantic with horror at the land on no regulation.

Who, what, where ,when and why? Five questions that are at the heart of our trade. Answer those questions in relation to any news story, and we're doing our jobs as journalists. They underpin everything we do, what we write in a newspaper or online, what we say on TV or on the radio.

It feels to me however that one of those questions we sometimes need to ask of ourselves. Why? It doesn't have to be everyday or all the time but given the power we have, it's important. What is the point of the media in a democracy? What are we here for? We can influence massive societal changes. Indirectly we even wield political power, are able to influence policy, perhaps even are able to help change governments. And with power, as we're all well aware, comes great responsibility.

But who should police this? Is it enough to let the industry itself be the gatekeeper of how far a broadcaster or newspaper should go in trying to make a profit or build an audience or are independent regulators the only way to ensure media companies use the power they have wisely?

Let's focus on broadcasting and contrast the situation here in the UK, where there is a robust and for some choking regulatory framework, with the United States, where oversight in one crucial respect is non-existent: the requirement to fairly represent the views of opposing sides in news and current affairs broadcasts. Could that lack of a check on how America does news actually imperil democracy itself?

America: the Great Frontier?

I love America and its endless possibilities. In the 1990s I was the BBC West Coast correspondent based in Los Angeles, but I frequently made trips to Washington. I will never forget the first time I went inside the White House. I was in awe to be at the heart of global power. I later spent quite a bit of time at 1600 Pennsylvania Avenue as the full time BBC Washington Correspondent while George W. Bush was in residence. I've covered every Presidential election since 1996, including Joe Biden's recent victory.

The fact that the richest democracy on the planet cannot quite get it right and promote the interests of all its citizens is what's endlessly fascinating about America.

Opinion pays on US TV, on British TV impartiality rules

The US opinion hosts like Sean Hannity of Fox News and Andersen Cooper of CNN are why people switch on cable TV. It's the opinion hosts who can mould and shape minds, with many millions of viewers every week. They make the money for the networks, because their followers are loyal and TV news providers in America aren't under any legal obligation to be fair and impartial.

Broadcasters in the UK, however, are forced to be honest, fair, and impartial in their news coverage in order to hold a licence. The rules come under section five of the regulator *Ofcom*'s codes-covering due impartiality and accuracy and opinions. Similar rules did exist in America, but were thrown out more than 30 years ago when Ronald Reagan was President, and attempts since to revive the legislation have always stalled on the altar of the First Amendment – the right to free speech.

In the US you can say what you like – your opinion is protected, and you can use all your power and might to beam that opinion right across the land, without giving any counter arguments, without reporting the opposing point of view.

Opinion can be dressed up as news.

Whom do you trust on TV?

There are many in America horrified by the opinion hosts on both the right and the left, whether it be Fox News or MSNBC. Yet a study last year[1] showed that both channels were in the top five of the most trusted news brands for viewers, symbolising the country's political polarisation. It's clear many Americans want their views affirmed, not challenged…

But there is absolutely no reason why an independent regulator would materially damage the consumer. The number three brand in that survey is PBS, the Public Broadcasting Service, whose nightly News*hour* was deemed in a study by the University of California to be "the most centrist news program on television and the closest news show to holding a truly objective stance." That's because it has to be fair and balanced as PBS is technically not a network but a programme distributor that provides television content and related services to its member stations across America in blue states and red states.

But what's the news brand that beats them all – Fox News, PBS, Bloomberg, and MSNBC – when it comes to public trust? It's the heavily regulated British Broadcasting Corporation. The BBC, subject to independent rules on impartiality and accuracy is the most trusted news brand in America.

The figures are revealing, and clearly suggest that an ambition to be impartial, watched over by independent regulation, does make a difference for the better in helping to increase levels of public trust.

Trust the BBC?

The BBC isn't perfect by any means. Trust levels are under pressure especially after the terribly divisive Brexit campaign. Its system of funding is under scrutiny like never before, and the giant tech companies with seemingly bottomless pockets of cash are now big media players. Yet the news division of this ancient institution, which will be 100 years old next year, still commands levels of trust many other media organisations would die for.

Research in 2020 by the independent think tank the Reuters Institute for The Study of Journalism at Oxford University[2] suggests the BBC is the most popular source of news in the UK among both Conservative

---

[1] https://brandkeys.com/wp-content/uploads/2019/06/073018Mediapost-TVs-Most-Trusted-News-Brands.pdf.

[2] https://reutersinstitute.politics.ox.ac.uk/risj-review/bbc-under-scrutiny-heres-what-research-tells-about-its-role-uk.

and Labour voters and among Leave and Remain voters even after Brexit. This research showed that while the BBC is slightly less trusted by people who identify with the political right than people in the centre and on the left, it is still as trusted on the right as the major Conservative newspapers.

Public service broadcasting, properly regulated, helps ensure people see more diverse news, reduces the gap between the most and the least politically engaged, and plays a crucial role in helping prevent all manner of issues being viewed through a partisan and political lens. Not to put too fine a point on it, in its own way, the BBC helps bind the country together.

No trust in US journalism...

And that is America's fundamental problem that I witnessed first-hand during last year's Presidential election – the trust deficit at the heart of American democracy. For the first time ever, Edelman's annual trust barometer shows fewer than half of all Americans have trust in traditional media. 56% of Americans believe journalists and reporters lie, and 58% believe most news organisations are more concerned with supporting an ideology or political position, rather than informing the public. This is a state of affairs that has serious consequences for the fabric of US society and the future of American democracy.

The storming of the US Capitol Building on Jan 6 this year shamed America, but was partly the logical conclusion of a toxic media environment with no rules, promoting public distrust. It was one consequence of a media free for all and was years in the making. And where there is a void of fact and truth and public trust, conspiracy theories can live and breed.

Will the UK follow the USA?

But in the UK, despite the public's overwhelming confidence in the BBC and other public service news providers like ITN and Channel 4 News silo thinking, the need to have your opinions re-enforced rather than challenged is on the march.

I travelled around the country during the 2019 election campaign from County Durham to Southampton, Enniskillen to Pembrokeshire, and I came across people on the Right who'd be very happy to get their news from a UK equivalent of Fox News, and some on the Left who'd be very happy to watch a British equivalent of MSNBC. For them, *Ofcom*, in simply carrying out the will of Parliament, suddenly becomes "the oppressive state" – somehow unaccountable and anti-Democratic. These might be some of the very same people who'd defend the primacy of Parliament in any discussion about the EU, or so-called "activist judges."

Why we do it?

I began with thoughts on who, what, where, when and why, the basic ingredients of our trade as journalists. And I suggested that from time to time, we needed to ask ourselves, why do we do what we do?

There might actually be a point to independent regulators, because a clear and transparent set of rules and guidelines that everyone can follow and everyone can see increases public trust. The facts are plain. Public confidence in an unregulated media, falls well below the level of confidence for a media that's regulated.

I'll conclude with the words contained within the Fairness Doctrine, now consigned to history in America, but alive and well in the regulations of *Ofcom*:

"Licensees must not use their stations 'for the private interest, whims or caprices of licensees, but in a manner which will serve the community generally as a whole. Broadcasters must provide adequate coverage of public issues, and ensure that coverage, fairly represents opposing views."

The maintenance of democracy and a just and fair society. That is why, I think, we do what we do as broadcast journalists.

This is an edited version of a Speech in honour of Sir Harold Evans given on March 11th 2021.It was supported by The Society of Editors and the London Press Club. Produced by John Mair See the whole speech at https://youtu.be/VucKN2112eU

About the Contributor

Clive Myrie is a BBC News Presenter and Correspondent of thirty years standing. He is the 2021 RTS Television Journalist of the year and the 2021 RTS Network News Presenter of the year.

Section One
Ofcom A Watchdog With Teeth Or Just Gums?

John Mair

How has *Ofcom* performed after its difficult birth? David Elstein is a walking television historian, and has held very senior positions at ITV, Channel Five and Sky for over 45 years. This has given him plenty of opportunity to see the whittling away of public service obligations by light touch – perhaps better described as soft touch regulation by the IBA, ITC and *Ofcom*. The commercial ITV companies too were keen to push back the obligations (and cost) of news, religion, children's and more. The BBC joined in their shadow in the rush from PSB.

Today, away from the news, few PSB programmes come from the terrestrial commercial companies. The BBC holds up its end but defines PSB in a rather catholic way. Being supervised by *Ofcom* puts some lead in their pencil.

Elstein's essay, '**A (not so) brief history of PSB Time'** is a tour de force. Future historians of broadcasting and culture will go to it as a seminal document of the decline from a 'Golden Age' of four channels to an age of plenty, where streamers take the British public subscriptions by the million and the British terrestrial broadcasters are backed into specialist corners.

Janice Hughes is a specialist on the other 'dirty' side of *Ofcom*: the regulation of telecoms that was its initial raison d'etre as *Oftel*. The 800 strong body today started off subletting part of her office in Victoria. In '***Ofcom* In the Beginning'**, she sees *Ofcom* as having regulated telephony well, especially after the BT monopoly was broken. The UK mobile phone market is very competitive and getting cheaper for the consumer. But it has been less good at the big bits – providing large capacity to homes/offices and rural broadband. It may have squared the technocratic phone circle but has it the experience and expertise to regulate the tech titan?

Simon Albury is another eminence grise of British broadcasting. A former *Granada* producer, he helped to win an ITV franchise – *Meridian* – then became CEO of the prestigious Royal Television Society for 12 years. Today he is a free man concentrating on trying to make British TV more diverse. But he wants it to go back to its and his roots, and create a whole new series of Granadas. In **'Time for *Ofcom* to re-visit and re-invent Granada-land?'** Albury calls on *Ofcom* to be the midwife of this re-birth.

Marcus Ryder is working hard to create diversity in television in conjunction with his friend Sir Lenny Henry. But in his essay he comes at it in a very unusual way – looking not at race and gender, but at market shape through an economist's eyes. He introduces the idea of monopsony – few buyers, many sellers – for tv programmes. He argues this needs to be reformed through diversity in purchase. As he puts it: **'Lack of diversity is a market failure – that's why it needs a strong regulator'**.

Lastly in this section is a voice departing from the liberal consensus. Robin Aitken is an unashamed social conservative. He writes for the *Daily Telegraph* after all! In **'*Ofcom*: a *Naked Attraction* to liberals?'** he sees *Ofcom* as not just a censor of outre political views, but as also allowing 'outre-sexual' programmes like *Naked Attraction* on Channel 4. Dacre's time at *Ofcom* cannot come soon enough for him.

Watchdog or toothless wonder? You decide.

Chapter Six

A (not so) brief history of PSB Time

David Elstein – former head of programmes at Thames and BSkyB, and CEO of Channel 5 – casts his unique eye on *Ofcom*'s part in the long, slow decline of UK Public Service Broadcasting.

I wrote my post-graduate thesis on the concept of public service broadcasting (PSB) 57 years ago, under the supervision of Stuart Hall and Richard Hoggart, two key figures in the study of contemporary culture.

Hoggart had been the driving force behind the 1962 Pilkington Report, whose harsh verdict on the performance of ITV – deemed to be guilty of vulgar consumerism – had led to wholesale reform of the regulation of the commercial service. It was the constraints of limited spectrum that shaped the concept of PSB in those days. Just as the BBC's monopoly status had imposed duties of public service – provision of information, education and entertainment – so the BBC/ITV duopoly could only be justified if those in control supplied high quality content and a degree of high-mindedness.

Pilkington rejected the whole idea of consumer choice, opposing the development of cable and satellite. Competition was frowned upon, and too much provision discouraged. Even allowing broadcasters to transmit through the night was decades away. ITV and the BBC agreed – or were told – not to undermine audiences for God, children's or Monday evening current affairs: choice was restricted by pitting like against like. Scarcity ruled.

Television's 'Golden Age'?

Once reformed, ITV's regulatory system delivered what is now seen as a golden age of PSB in the 1970s and 1980s. All ITV licensees were required to contribute where they could, but in any event to fund and commit, to network quotas for news, current affairs, adult education, schools, children's programmes, religion, arts and documentaries; to meet individual local quotas for regional news, features and current affairs output. More importantly, the quality of this content was judged, at network and regional level, by expert regulators, who wrote annual reports on performance. These could alert potential rivals to any incumbents judged to be falling below the required standards. Such challengers could then offer themselves as replacements at the regular 'beauty contests' for renewal of ITV licences.

This ITV cornucopia of PSB provoked a strong response from the BBC, which suddenly discovered that competition for quality was the best thing that had ever happened to it. Nor was it just in the designated 'public service' genres that this serendipity worked: in drama, in comedy, in light entertainment and in factual series both broadcast systems responded to emulative pressure to excel.

When Channel 4 was launched in 1982, funded by advertising but not required by its owners (us) to deliver profits or dividends, another swathe of competitive excellence was introduced, and new PSB output quotas came into being. And even though there was no provision for Channel 4 to face competition for its licence, the regulator – first the Independent Broadcasting Authority, then the Independent Television Commission – still issued qualitative judgments alongside the counting of the hours.

What's this Channel Fo(u)r?

The first version of Channel 4 was remarkably similar to the structure Pilkington had recommended for ITV: the schedule being funded by a levy on those selling the new channel's airtime (the ITV companies, keeping their advertising monopoly as compensation for not being awarded the ITV2 they had been promised), with programme suppliers held at arm's length from a central commissioning body whose non-executive directors were appointed by the IBA.

Within that protective environment, and while satellite and cable take-up was in its early phase, Channel 4 could adopt a whole range of PSB objectives, with extensive quotas: news, current affairs, schools (transferred as an obligation from ITV), formal education, religion, multicultural output, documentaries and arts, in addition to strict limits on repeats, especially in peak-time, a contribution to the National Film Archive and – uniquely – a training levy as a percentage of turnover.

When Channel 4 secured the right to sell its own airtime – as a result of one of the unexpected recommendations of the 1986 Peacock

Report on the funding of the BBC– the consequent rising tide of revenue financed significant increases in the programme budget, allowing the level of quotas to be steadily expanded.

Technology rules? Or the market? Or the law?

The decline in delivery of PSB, especially in the commercial sector, is routinely dated to the changes in technology which eroded – and eventually ended – spectrum scarcity: the spread of cable and satellite technology, the adoption of digital broadcasting, greater competition for viewers and advertising revenues, the undermining of the value of "gifted" spectrum (which was seen as underpinning PSB delivery by the beneficiaries of the "gift"); and finally the spread of broadband and the rise of the streamers.

Yet this was neither an incremental nor an inevitable process. Until the switch to digital, the impact of cable and satellite on viewing and revenues was modest. Even digital broadcasting proved to be quite a limited threat, with ministers choosing to counter Sky's adoption of digital satellite with the allocation of additional digital terrestrial spectrum to the incumbent PSB broadcasters. The BBC, ITV, Channel 4 and the newly-arrived Five (subject to very modest PSB obligations, given its marginal commercial prospects) rapidly expanded their provision of channels, thereby successfully limiting any loss of viewing to the hundreds of satellite services that digital transmission enabled.

But for PSB content as such, this strategy proved devastating. Although the new channels from the BBC were required to fulfil PSB purposes, those launched by ITV, Channel 4 and Five bore almost no such obligations. Yet their success in winning viewers came almost entirely at the expense of the channels subject to PSB rules.

Channel 4's portfolio of channels quickly achieved a viewing share of nearly 11% – but that was the viewing share of Channel 4 alone before the launch of digital terrestrial TV. With the benefit of cross-promotion from the main channel, the new siblings captured half of Channel 4's viewing – without offering any public service content. Indeed, the most successful of these services, E4, consisted overwhelmingly of repeats and US imports, putting it in regular danger of breaching the most basic obligation facing such channels: that at least 50% of their output consists of EU works.

Auctioning off the family silver?

Likewise, the decline of PSB in ITV can be traced back, not to pressure on advertising revenues, but to the auctioning of licences, as recommended by Peacock (another diversion from its stated remit of advising on the financing of the BBC). This backfired in (mostly) predictable ways. The first auction was so badly designed and destabilising that ministers and regulators agreed there would never be another. Instead, high bidders quickly whittled away their contractual payments. There could be no more 'beauty contests' once franchises effectively became freeholds. And as the ITV franchises consolidated into a single public company outside Scotland, the ability of any regulator to hold a licensee to its obligations became increasingly tenuous.

Change the law, bend the rules?

Yet what decisively pulled the plug on PSB was legislation, not technology. The Communications Act of 2003 merged a number of regulators into a single body: The Office for Communications, or *Ofcom*. The thinking of the Blair government was that as broadcasting and telecommunications moved from overlap to merger, a combined regulator was needed to manage issues that would arise. As it turned out, there has been almost no instance of *Ofcom* exercising its dual oversight. Telecommunications supervision sits separately within the organisation from broadcast regulation. Crucially, the quality control expertise built up over decades within the IBA and ITC disappeared.

As ITV franchises would no longer be subject to quality requirements, the absence of such expertise was never an issue. Indeed, the 2003 Act explicitly abandoned almost the entirety of the PSB quota regime. Instead, only news and current affairs were retained in what became tier 2 of the regulatory regime (tier 1 covered broader duties applying to all licensees). All other content requirements were assigned to tier 3, which effectively made them voluntary. Quotas for independent commissions and productions from outside London were easy to meet.

As it happens, the newly solidified ITV plc had already flexed its muscles in fending off regulation, when it relegated its main news bulletin, News At Ten, to the edge of peak-time for no less than nine years, ignoring the protests of the then regulator, the ITC.

Gate open, ITV drives through...

Under *Ofcom*, ITV moved quickly and ruthlessly to eliminate as much of its old-style PSB content as the new legislation allowed. A downturn in advertising in 2008 was offered as grounds for significantly reducing the amount spent on regional output. Now that the merged ownership of regional licences made it possible to share material across ITV, *Ofcom* was offered Hobson's choice: allow ITV to make savings by sharing, or see all regions reduce their output. The cuts were made. Since then, ITV has distributed £5 billion in dividends, but the lost output has never been restored.

Next, ITV started to cut back on children's programming in its schedule, which was allowed under tier 3 provided such changes were "not material" and were made after consulting *Ofcom* (whose opinion, however hostile, could legally be ignored). After three "non-material" cuts, children's programmes disappeared to a niche channel, CITV. The BBC – not at that stage regulated by *Ofcom*, and not faced by any threat to advertising income – followed suit, exiling all children's programmes from its main channels to the ghettoes of CBeebies and CBBC (though at least the BBC continued to make new children's programmes). This mirroring was to become a familiar phenomenon.

By the time ITV decided to axe its arts and nearly all its religious programming (save for a church service at Christmas), *Ofcom* had lost the will to resist. The cuts were clearly material, but there had been "consultation", so *Ofcom* acquiesced.

...followed by Channel 4

Channel 4 now took advantage of the 2003 Act to issue a "statement of media policy" of inordinate length and minimal consequence, which allowed it to abandon virtually all the impressive PSB quotas that had distinguished its first two decades of broadcasting. Tier 2 requirements kept peak-time news and current affairs alive, but the 16 hours a week of formal education, schools, multicultural output and religion all disappeared, along with most serious documentaries and arts output (there was a time when Channel 4 not only broadcast whole operas but commissioned them).

To rub salt in the wound, Channel 4 proceeded to categorise any factual programme as "educational", claiming to broadcast 50 hours a week of "education". For this shameful outcome, we can only blame

Ofcom, as the 2003 Act specifically requires Channel 4 to make "a significant contribution of programmes of an educational nature *and* other programmes of educational value". The pre-*Ofcom* regulators would have known what that language meant.

The old requirements for first-run UK-originated (FRUKO) programmes (60% of the schedule, 80% in peak time) have been dropped. Repeats regularly constitute 60% of the schedule and could in theory – apart from news and current affairs requirements – fill the entire schedule without breaching Channel 4*'s Ofcom* licence. The decline in delivery of what *Ofcom* itself called at-risk genres, combined with the halving of its audience share, meant that consumption of old PSB-style content through watching Channel 4 amounts on average to one minute per day per viewer.

The "statement of media policy" provision in the 2003 Act allows broadcasters like Channel 4 to self-set and self-mark notions of PSB output, which simply have to meet *Ofcom*'s own baggy definitions of public service "purposes and characteristics". These tests cannot be failed. Meanwhile, the BBC, too, has shed much of its formal education output, and moved schools' content online (from where elements were recently retrieved to support the BBC's much-praised contribution to home schooling during the epidemic). That, it transpired, was only part of the story. As *Ofcom* was to report, the decline in spending by ITV on nations and regions content of £41m per annum from 2004 to 2008 was closely matched by the BBC*'s* decline in annual spend of £34m (after 2008, ITV cut a further £70m a year).

Ofcom 'reviews': a watchdog with no teeth

When *Ofcom* was created, it was given the task of monitoring PSB delivery. It also embarked on a review of the whole system, perhaps influenced by the findings of the first of its successive reports on the state of PSB, as laid down in the legislation. Over the years, these reports documented an accelerating decline (other than in national and international news) in supply of the key genres of output previously regarded as PSB: regional news, current affairs, children's programming, religion, ethics, arts, documentaries, adult education and schools.

By 2006, it was already obvious that the combination of technological and legislative change had removed the old levers that had allowed regulators to require delivery of these genres by ITV, Channel 4 and

Five; and that the BBC, for reasons of its own, beyond the scope of *Ofcom*, was reducing its own supply of these genres. So, *Ofcom* came up with the idea of a Public Service Publisher, which would use central funds to commission and publish new public service content.

This seemed to be a variation of yet another of the Peacock Report's recommendations: that a Public Service Broadcasting Commission be created to focus solely on the creation of PSB material, in parallel with the phasing out of the licence fee as BBC financing was switched to subscription. The difference in *Ofcom's* approach – other than a modish embrace of online content as part of the PSB system – was that the PSP would create its own distribution system, separate from the existing terrestrial channels; something Peacock thought unnecessary.

Unsurprisingly, the PSP was criticised on grounds of expense and of wasteful duplication of distribution effort. There was never any likelihood that – over and above maintaining the licence fee – the government would supply the £300 million a year that *Ofcom* estimated as the cost of the whole package. Subsequently, *Ofcom* came back with a lower cost for its proposals, but by then the PSP was dead in the water. A chastened *Ofcom* never returned to structural change.

A doleful tale...

Yet *Ofcom*'s statutory monitoring of PSB delivery told an increasingly doleful tale of woe. The 2009 report logged a 28% decline in education output across the system in just 5 years, accompanied by declines of 32% in arts, 34% in religion, 39% in regional content and 48% in children's programming. The transfer of children's to niche channels – by both ITV and the BBC – resulted in the share of children's viewing devoted to actual children's programming falling from 32% to 12%. As the at-risk genres became harder to find, viewing of them fell even faster than provision of them: 52% for music, 58% for arts and 70% for education. Even supply of categories outside the "endangered species" group – such as high-risk drama and comedy – were noted by *Ofcom* as diminishing: within a decade, ITV's provision of drama was to drop from 7 hours a week to 2, and comedy to disappear almost altogether.

Each *Ofcom* review recorded further decline, in output and expenditure, across the public service categories. Arts, current affairs, nations and regions, children's (described by *Ofcom* as "a vitally important part of PSB", but where only the BBC continued to be active): the pattern was consistent, with the BBC mimicking the commercial sector's behaviour in nearly all genres. In two areas, declared *Ofcom* in 2015, "provision has all but ceased: religion and ethics (down 58% since 1988) and formal education (down 77% since 1998)".

Despite this cataloguing of failure, *Ofcom* felt unable to intervene, as the 2003 legislation (effectively re-confirmed by the 2010 Digital Economy Act) had removed its teeth. Compelled to judge by the new rules, *Ofcom* concluded that "the PSB channels have generally fulfilled the PSB remit": in other words, those in the commercial sector had submitted a statement of media policy, and the BBC (which belatedly became answerable to *Ofcom* for its PSB delivery) also passed the relevant tests. Indeed, *Ofcom* noted "a wide range of learning and educational content" on BBC TV, even though only 0.01% of its output is classified as education.

System failing, so change the criteria

With its big idea having run into the ground, and with its reporting of PSB genre decline at odds with its lack of power to do anything about it, *Ofcom* decided to change the terms of the PSB argument. Instead of a solemn counting of the hours as defined by the past, the test of PSB would be the system's contribution to UK origination. "High levels of original content," said *Ofcom* CEO Ed Richards, would now "meet the public purposes of PSB".

This may have seemed a safe bet in 2004, when the 5 PSB channels (plus S4C) accounted for 97% of all spend on first run UK origination (FRUKO), and even in 2008 at the time of Richards' intervention. However, by 2017, the PSBs represented just 44% of FRUKO. Sky had boosted its non-sport origination budget to £500m pa, and its *"Patrick Melrose"* and *"Chernobyl"* won successive BAFTAs for best drama series. *Ofcom* calculated that BBC TV's actual spending on content was far less than the BBC itself claimed: and that figure - £1.852bn in 2004 – had dropped to £1.177bn by 2017, continuing to fall after then. The amount for 2021 will be well below £1bn, excluding sport. At the same time, content spend by ITV *and* Channel 4 has fallen from £1.5bn to less than £1bn, again, excluding sport.

the £3.364bn (£2.85bn excluding sport) that the PSB system had spent on FRUKO in 2004 had collapsed to less than £2bn in 2021. Yet *Ofcom*, which had expressed "concern" about the system in its second PSB review, then decided it "remained strong" in its third review, and concluded in its fourth review that it had "generally fulfilled" its obligations, despite spending just 0.52% of its meagre budgets on children's, 0.25% on arts and 0.08% on religion.

Enter the streamers...

In the meantime, *Netflix* and then *Amazon* began investing hundreds of millions of pounds a year in UK production, providing budgets that dwarfed anything the PSB channels could muster. It was in High End TV (HETV) production – which the PSB channels had urged governments to support with generous tax breaks – that the disparity between the performance of the PSBs and that of the new arrivals became most painfully apparent.

By 2020, the PSB system was contributing just 15% of all the cost of HETV (which is predominantly drama). Between 2008 and 2018, the PSBs cut their drama hours from 627 a year to 338, and that figure continues to decline. Drama now commands just 10% of PSB budgets. In the last week of March 2021, the whole of BBC TV offered just one hour of originated first-run non-soap drama *("Line of Duty")*, but 21 hours of quizzes, game shows and elimination contests.

Feel the width

If we want to understand the huge surge in take-up of subscription services – over 80% of UK households now enjoy some combination of *Netflix, Amazon Prime, Disney+,* Sky *and Virgin Media* – we need only look at the relative offerings of the terrestrial channels and the streamers in terms of drama, which constitutes 2% of terrestrial output, but nearly 60% of what is available on *Netflix and Amazon Prime* (31,000 hours between them, not including movies).

The BBC's response? That the PSB system delivers 32,000 hours of UK-made programming a year, compared with less than 250 from the streamers. Never mind the quality, feel the width! As *Ofcom* points out, more than half of this PSB output is actually live news and current affairs, with minimal archive value. Even the non-PSB commercial broadcasters in the UK deliver over 22,000 of FRUKO amongst their 140,000 hours of programming every year, much of it available on free-to-air services. And Sky News is not slow to point out that its budget is ring-fenced till 2028, while the BBC is cutting hundreds of jobs in its news division.

Ofcom also tells us that *Netflix* currently offers nearly 800 hours of UK-made programming, virtually all at the upper end of the quality scale. Currently, the streamers (*now joined by Disney+*) *and* Sky are competing for vast amounts of studio space in the UK, as they step up their investment in UK-made programming. It is only a matter of time before the streamers alone are spending more than the BBC on FRUKO, and the streamers, Sky, *HBO, Disney, AMC and Hulu* more between them than the whole PSB system.

But we are British!

The latest fall-back position of the PSB system – genres having been abandoned, the highest quality long since conceded to US subscriber services, and FRUKO spend no longer a claim to distinctiveness – is "Britishness", as calculated in a recent Enders Analysis (hereafter EA) paper, and cited by John Whittingdale MP, now number two in the Department for Culture he used to head.

Even if patriotism were not, as Dr Johnson reminds us, the last refuge of the scoundrel, the methodology used by EA should certainly give us pause. Apparently, neither *"Bridgerton"* nor *"The Crown"*, both from Netflix, meets the "Britishness" test, despite their obvious claims. *"Bridgerton"* is disqualified because it has an American producer and is based on novels written by an American. Presumably, all those Henry James classic BBC serials would fail the test, too, not to mention the *Armchair Theatre and Wednesday Play* productions overseen by the Canadian, Sydney Newman.

"Maigret", in both its incarnations (and likewise *"Van Der Valk"*), would also be disqualified, along with *"War and Peace", "Anna Karenina", "A Suitable Boy", "Chernobyl", "The Serpent"*, and anything based on Conrad, Shaw, Beckett, Colm ("Brooklyn") Toibin or Atwood. *"The Crown"*, we are told by EA, contains "relatively few British terms, expressions, reference points or idioms". What, we might ask, does it contain? By contrast, *"Coronation Street"* tops the qualifiers' list, apparently scoring with phrases like "a Cara Delevingne lookalike contest".

I enjoy Corrie, but the notion that it represents anything other than a fantasy version of "Britishness" is itself fanciful. Half the Street has spent time in jail, at least ten murderers and serial killers have lived in that handful of houses, and for the first three months of 2021 the show occupied a twilight zone where shops, cafés, pubs, hairdressers and restaurants entertain customers indoors, whilst the cast – in order for filming to remain compliant with Covid rules – stand or sit six feet apart from each other, even when sharing a meal, some wearing masks, others not. The epidemic itself has yet to claim a Corrie victim.

As for that most celebrated of current BBC drama series, *Line of Duty*, although it is shot in Belfast, you would have no idea of that, or indeed of anywhere in the UK it might have been located. It is a drama devoid of setting, remote from any actual policing activity and filled with its own jargon, which even falls short of the Cara Delevingne test. How "British" is that?

The Age of Relativism

This latest "last stand" by supporters of the PSB status quo is more than foolish: it is embarrassing. But there is worse. As part of its latest consultation on what it now calls PSM (M for "media"), which closed in March, *Ofcom* volunteered the view that anything popular amounted to public service content, including soaps and shiny floor shows. Channel 4 told us that *"The Great British Bake Off"* is PSB. In this relativist world, the BBC can offer up as public service broadcasting *"Gordon Ramsay's Bank Balance" and "This Is My House"* (described by previewers as "thin entertainment from flimsy material" and "a piece of ill-thought-out fluff").

Meanwhile, EA dismisses "the likes of *Netflix*" as being "only interested in British productions that have global potential" (so much for *"The Dig"*). Indeed, EA seems not to understand the basic principle of a subscriber service, which is to offer range and excellence, drawn from multiple cultures. Maximizing audience size and share at any moment of time is a preoccupation of linear broadcasters, not of streamers, or even of the likes of HBO, AMC, Showtime or FX.

Relativism and Luddism...

The retreat into relativism is neither new nor unthinking. Jana Bennett, as Director of Television for the BBC in 2004, claimed *"The Weakest Link"* as PSB. For the BBC, *anything it chooses to broadcast is by definition PSB.* That way, the rational approach by Peacock – that public service content is what the market cannot provide, and therefore needs public funding, whilst everything else can be paid for, or not, by the consumer, exercising choice – can be evaded.

When Peacock recommended the auctioning of ITV franchises, he did so with the intention that, during the transfer of the BBC from licence fee funding to subscription, the auction proceeds would fund public service content. Indeed, former chairmen and Directors-General of the BBC asserted that the BBC itself, the licence fee and, indeed, any public intervention in broadcasting was posited on market failure. What they were reluctant to accept was that the BBC provided a mixture of public service content and content readily replicable in the market.

Of course, the BBC, like ITV and Channel 4, still provides many hundreds of hours a year of high-quality programming, in amongst the many thousands of hours of ho-hum stuff. That the debate about the future of PSB (sorry, PSM) revolves around how to shore up the privileged position enjoyed by the PSBs on old-style distribution systems is as much a failure of politicians and *Ofcom* to acknowledge how far PSB delivery has withered over the last twenty years as of those who were meant to be delivering it.

"Punish the TV set makers!"

The BBC is even now proposing that manufacturers of smart TVs build in mechanisms to ensure prominence for its offerings at least equal to that for Netflix and Sky, or face massive fines. This, of course, is the BBC that fought successfully to block Peacock's main recommendation – that new TV sets be required to build in a peri-television socket that would simplify access to subscription services (as was the case in France and Italy) – and also insisted on the removal of conditional access modules from set-top boxes when it took over digital terrestrial TV, so as to block the pathway to replacing the licence fee with subscription.

The relativist approach to PSB is part and parcel of that strain of Luddism. The BBC argues today that a switch to subscription is impossible until the last UK household is connected to high-speed broadband: an absurd position if it is recognised that all BBC public service content will remain publicly funded and freely available on terrestrial TV, even after its entertainment output transfers to subscription (which in turn would be easily accessible by practically all households, even if some might need to make cheap and simple upgrades to their reception equipment if they wished to subscribe).

The signs are that politicians – and *Ofcom* – are prepared to back this latest piece of obstructionism, with the Commons Select Committee on

Culture (whose latest report on PSB makes no mention of quality control in its 63 pages) even nominating 2038 as the earliest that the licence fee will fade into history. How ironic that this will be more than fifty years since Alasdair Milne, on behalf of the BBC, told Peacock that subscription was the best alternative to the licence fee.

Yet Peacock – for all his clear-sightedness and logical thinking – did not see far enough ahead. He did not anticipate the rise of Sky, or even the possible launch of Channel 5. The ITV spectrum that was worth £340m a year in the 1990s is now worth barely £25m. The tiny pot of contestable funding for public service content – the £20m a year set aside in 2016 – is bitterly opposed by the BBC, as undermining support for the licence fee (on what evidence, is not disclosed). *Ofcom*, once the champion of contestability, is now silent on the subject.

Ofcom and the BBC

Having at long last been given oversight of the BBC*'s* public service performance, *Ofcom* in its first report noted several years of decline in spending on FRUKO, "significantly fewer individual titles", "a decrease in at-risk genre spend, continuing a downward trend since 2010", that 62% of those surveyed felt BBC delivery of public service purposes was "weak", that most "learning" was "informal", that only 57% of respondents thought the BBC "innovative" and that consumer satisfaction was higher amongst Sky customers, and much higher amongst *Netflix* and *Amazon* customers. Nonetheless, according to *Ofcom*, the BBC was meeting its public service obligations.

The streamers ain't done yet...

The truth is that we are barely half way through the rise of the streamers. Within two years, *Netflix, Disney and Amazon Prime* will have over 500 million subscribers worldwide. *Britbox*, both here and in the US, will be an industry footnote. The combined production budgets of the streamers will easily exceed £30 billion a year, rendering the BBC*'s* £1bn marginal: and that's before Apple gets its act together, as it surely must.

And the consumer is already drifting out of reach. The average 18-34year old spends 2 minutes a day with *iPlayer*, 40 minutes with *Netflix* and 64 minutes with YouTube. 16-24 year olds spend almost twice as much time with the streamers and *YouTube* as with live TV. A typical Channel 4 News bulletin attracts just 0.004% of the channel's favourite demographic, the 16-34s. A large proportion of that age group expect to have given up broadcast TV entirely within five years.

Some passionate supporters of the BBC were worried last year that a Johnson government would take an axe to the BBC. They should have been more worried by the likelihood that benign neglect will inflict more harm: as the years pass, as consumers adjust to the ever-increasing pace of technological change, so the PSB system will fade into history. Yet the need for content that the market cannot deliver remains strong, even as our main public broadcaster clings to a form of financing that intentionally fudges what is public service content and what is not, our regulatory regime remains weak, and our chief regulator settles for the easy life.

All the data contained in this article can be found in documents on the Ofcom website, including all annual reports on public service broadcasting, three reviews of public service broadcasting (2004, 2008 and 2014) plus a 4th review in a different format in 2019, and regular reports on the communications industries and consumer behaviour.

About the Contributor.

David Elstein joined the BBC in 1964, moving to ITV in 1968. He has worked on *The World At War, Weekend World*, and *This Week*. He left to start Brook Productions when Channel 4 launched in 1982, returned to Thames TV as Director of Programmes (1986-92), and was later Head of Programming at BSkyB and CEO of Channel 5. He also served as chair of the National Film and Television School and the British Screen Advisory Council, as well as on the board of Virgin Media for five years.

Chapter Seven

Ofcom: In the beginning

> **Janice Hughes CBE was there at the creation. Working for Oftel then *Ofcom*. She looks back over the last quarter of a century of regulation of broadcasting and telephony.**

I was involved with the creation of both *Oftel* and *Ofcom*. In 1984 I was the MD of the Economists Advisory Group, working closely on competition and pricing issues with Sir Bryan Carsberg, when he was invited to be the first Director General of *Oftel*. The privatisation of British Telecom (BT) and the formation of *Oftel* was an historic moment; the advent of competition in the telecoms sector thrust regulation into the limelight. In 1988 I worked on the Beesley/Laidlaw IEA Review, which judged that not enough had been done to maximise competition nor to spur BT into greater efficiency.[1]

The cosy duopoly of BT and Mercury held back the growth of the television, cable and the digital electronics industries and the underlying structure of the sector was deemed "flawed." In 1989 Beesley and Laidlaw argued that BT's position was "broadly the same" post regulation "as when it was a nationalised industry", and one might well argue today, that it still has an ongoing dominant de facto monopoly position.

Many of the Beesley/Laidlaw criticisms about the way that the regulatory framework was set up by the 1984 Telecommunications Act and *Oftel*, lie at the root of why today, the UK has one of the lowest gigabit fibre uptake rates of all the OECD countries, at just 18%. BT's effective monopoly of the fixed copper network was never seriously challenged, nor was it pressed by *Ofcom* to invest in full fibre. It is only now after 18 years of *Ofcom* that a regulatory framework is beginning to emerge to enable new investors to compete in constructing fibre networks. The UK is falling short just at the time when there is the

---

[1] 'The Future of Telecommunications, An Assessment of the Role of Competition in UK Policy', by Michael E. Beesley and Bruce Laidlaw, published by the Institute of Economic Affairs, 1989.

highest demand ever experienced for connectivity for streaming (*Disney+, Netflix, Amazon* etc) and a permanent shift to working from home. Millions of people and premises all over the country are desperately in need of greater connectivity but will not be connected to full gigabit fibre for many years to come.

Throughout the late eighties and nineties, *Oftel's* focus was on issuing mobile licences, creating competition within the mobile sector, and charging users for the radio spectrum. As a Director at CSP, we carried out the first major radio spectrum deregulation study, enabling the sale of the 3G mobile licences that led to the Government benefitting from a £22.5bn windfall in payments from the spectrum auction in 2000.[1]

From the IBA to *Ofcom* via Norman Tebbit's waste paper bin...

In the early days broadcast regulation came under the *IBA* for commercial TV with the BBC under the remit of the Home Office. I was invited by them to undertake a major review of the option of privatising the BBC.[2] The report's title was '*Subscription Television*', which gave a clear pointer as to where the report was designed to lead. Our quantitative analysis concluded that the commercial benefits were outweighed "by the loss of consumer welfare since some viewers would not subscribe to services now available to them."[3] While we waited to present our report in his ante chamber in the Home Office, Norman Tebbitt sent our document skidding across the table to the floor, when he learned that we had not recommended the privatisation of the BBC. He refused even to meet us after our nine months of work for him. He railed continuously against the BBC. Margaret Thatcher saw "the licence fee as a tax on television viewers whether or not they watched the BBC, and saw the BBC as both wasteful and, later on, politically suspect".[4]

---

[1] Deregulation of the Radio Spectrum in the UK, by CSP International, HMSO 1987.

[2] Subscription Television, A Study for the Home Office, by CSP International/Booz Allen, HMSO 1988.

[3] Broadcasting in the '90s: Competition, Choice and Quality, The Government's Plans for Broadcasting Legislation, Home Department HMSO 1988.

[4] Glenn Aylott, Transdiffusion Broadcasting System, The IBA since 1964, 2005.

During the 1990 BBC Charter Review, Thatcher said "I have fought three elections against the BBC and don't want to fight another against it." Lord Young, Minister, Secretary of State for Trade and Industry, came to our offices at that time suggesting that we modelled moving BBC *One* and *Two* onto the Murdoch satellite platform, but that did not fly at all in our analysis.

Thatcher took her revenge another way, applying the spectrum auction approach used in mobile telephony to ITV, enabling the Government to take billions of pounds out of the television and production sectors and transferring it to the Treasury. The 1991 franchise round was seen by many as the death of regional television (see David Elstein Ch 6 in this volume).

The birth of *Ofcom* in 2003

Ofcom was formally established on 29 December 2003 as a super regulator replacing five separate bodies: *Oftel, the ITC* (successor to the IBA), *the Radio Authority, the Radiocommunications Agency* and *the Broadcasting Standards Commission*. Stephen Carter, the first CEO, started the *Ofcom* operation in our Spectrum Strategy offices. He told us he found the atmosphere more tranquil than at his previous job at *NTL*, where shoes had been known to fly around the boardroom table. Emerging from cable TV, advertising at JWT and PR at Brunswick, Stephen had a long and challenging to-do list in front of him: optimising spectrum use and stimulating electronic communications services and competition, while at the same time making sure that TV and radio were of high quality and wide appeal and not harmful to viewers.

All the talk at the millennium was about convergence (between media and telecoms), digital TV and the rapid emergence of online services. *Ofcom* was warned that the five largest European internet economies were mere minnows in relation to America's new tech imperium and would need to be regulated with vision and foresight.[1] In terms of wealth per capita, Silicon Valley was the world leader. In much the same way that the great trading cities of the past like Carthage or Athens became catalysts for wealth, so too was Palo Alto in California. Could Europe ever catch up?

---

[1] *E-Britannia: The Communications Revolution*, published by the University of Luton, 2000.

Wireless regulation fared well in the noughties, stimulating competition and rapid growth amongst the mobile licensees. Fixed telecoms had a short burst of competition as the dot-com boom exploded but reverted to type when it collapsed, allowing BT to re-establish its dominant position over the network leading to the 30m customers it has today out of 27.8m UK households.[1]

Killing Kangaroo

Broadcasting fared less well, as regulators failed to grapple with the growth and dominance of digital media developed by the world's largest tech groups: *Amazon, Apple, Facebook, Google* and *Netflix.* In many ways *Ofcom* seemed to be holding back UK broadcasters while endorsing the Government's championing of *BT. Ofcom* referred a key (negative) decision to The Competition Commission who actively blocked *Project Kangaroo*, the rather modest TV platform proposed by the BBC, ITV and Channel 4. The playing field was tipped firmly against the UK broadcasters in favour of the big tech giants. BBC, ITV and Channel 4 were compelled to work separately in this rapidly emerging streaming market as less than minnows and they were forced to sell off *Kangaroo's* assets for a song in 2009. In its final incarnation as *Seesaw*, it was finally shut down by *Arqiva* in 2011. This was a huge relief to the global tech groups, as British television had rightly been revered and commercially admired around the world. *Kangaroo* had been a real competitive threat in the platform streaming market and that was now extinguished.

The battle over EPGs

Prior to the millennium, viewers largely depended on print guides such as the *Radio Times* and *TV Times* to find their way to programmes. Then they moved to onscreen guides to help their viewers navigate their way around hundreds of cable and satellite channels. Today there are millions of viewing options across television, social media and user generated content.

In 2013 *Ofcom* had the opportunity to regulate the Electronic Programme Guides (EPGs) for all the global on demand platforms such as *Samsung, Sony, Roku* and even *Google TV* which existed briefly at time, but it chose to regulate only linear TV channels within the UK. At

---

[1] Office of National Statistics 2020.

the time, linear viewing was still robust (and it did not help that *BARB*, who counted the number of viewers on behalf of the TV companies and advertisers, could not track viewing for the on-demand players, so no one really knew exactly how much viewing they accounted for), so it seemed as though this was not such a significant omission.

How different that looks today.

On top of this, regulators had already tied the television companies' hands behind their backs by preventing the creation of *Kangaroo*-a joint on demand platform in 2009. This made it even harder trying to compete with the global TV and entertainment platforms. Perhaps they can be forgiven for not foreseeing *Netflix's* astonishing strategic vision and determined execution in implementing their first £5bn plus content strategy. It's hard today to recall that *Netflix* only started investing in original programming at any scale, in 2013. It seems as though our regulators were well behind the internet and digital wave, hindering the public service and commercial broadcasters from adopting streaming and subscription services, while sidestepping regulation for the big tech groups and adding only a light touch of regulation against BT and harmful content on satellite channels.

Not all bad news

There have though been major regulatory successes. One is the extraordinary growth and international reach of our independent television production sector that has roots firmly in the 25% independent production quota and the Terms of Trade regulation, first put in place by the *ITC* in 2003 and subsequently overseen by *Ofcom*. The quota guaranteed independent producers a share of the output on the public service channels, creating a vibrant sector where fortunes have been made and lost. The UK now has a truly global sector focused on optimising IP, and several of these companies are valued in the hundreds of millions. In the 1990s the number of British programmes seen on US television networks could be counted on one hand, whereas today there are dozens of British programmes seen across a multitude of channels, with the likes of *Downton Abbey* and David Attenborough's *Frozen Planet* topping the charts.

However, it is hard not to agree with the recent DCMS Select Committee report on the Future of Public Service Broadcasting that "Public Service Broadcasters are being let down by out-of-date legislation". *Ofcom* needs a refit to reflect the overwhelming demand for giganet connectivity and the content that is streamed over public service and commercial television channels and new media platforms.

It is clear that governments everywhere are preparing for a fundamental reset of their relationships with global tech players. Australia is likely to prove to be the first of many government attempts to assert a measure of control over the new media platforms. They will compel the tech giants to reflect local needs and concerns, control egregiously harmful content and support healthy local media ecosystems. All the things that public service broadcasting was set up to deliver. The UK Government must face up to the fact that it is going to have to regulate the tech giants. In 2018, then DCMS Secretary of State Jeremy Wright MP announced that the UK's creative sectors were now worth £268bn, up from £100bn in 2016. He stated that our creative industries "were outperforming the wider UK economy and we're doing all we can to support the sector's talent and entrepreneurship, as we build a Britain that is fit for the future."[1]

To be effective, therefore *Ofcom* needs the right regulatory mandate from the Government to enable it to fulfil this more ambitious role and to level the playing field between British broadcasters tipped against them by the tech giants. This is the urgent and immediate task for legislators as they create a new legislative framework to guide *Ofcom*'s oversight of the media and telecoms arena and *Ofcom* then needs to action it.

About the Contributor

Janice Hughes is currently a founder director of a new gigabit fibre network company, Graphite Strategy. She has had a front row seat at the creation and development of the UK's independent regulators *Oftel* and *Ofcom*. She was MD of the Economists Advisory Group, managing an eminent group of academics including Sir Bryan Carsberg, who then moved to become the first Director General of *Oftel*, the precursor to *Ofcom*. She then became a specialist consultant to the telecoms and media sectors, first at CSP, then as lead Partner heading Booz Allen & Hamilton's European Telecoms practice, before founding Spectrum Strategy Consultants and growing it to over 100 consultants in nine countries around the world. She played a leading role within the

---

[1] Britain's creative industries are now worth £268bn, Press Release DCMS, 28 November 2018.

DCMS's Creative Industries Taskforce alongside Paul Smith and Lord Puttnam, undertaking the first ever statistical review that demonstrated that the sector was worth more than £100bn, not far behind that of the financial services sector. In 2018 the DCMS announced that these creative sectors were now worth £268bn.

Chapter Eight

'Time for *Ofcom* to re-visit and re-invent Granada-land?'

"More money is needed but *Ofcom*'s jobsworth mindset will let down public service media" says Simon Albury former Chief Executive Officer of the Royal Television Society.

"As you read these words, some scrofulous tunnel rat in public office is busy selling your best interests down the road. It might be happening at your town council, zoning board, water district, or county commission — but it is happening."[1]

Words published on March 12, 2021, from novelist Carl Hiaasen's valedictory column for the Miami Herald.

"That's what happens when hometown journalism fades — neighbourhood stories don't get reported until it's too late, after the deal's gone down. Most local papers are gasping for life, and if they die it will be their readers who lose the most."

What is true for Miami journalism holds for the UK too.

We are at an interesting moment. Covid has swept away assumptions for daily living, for economic management, for political priorities - and *Ofcom*, the media regulator, is undertaking a review on "how to maintain and strengthen public service broadcasting across the next decade and beyond" and options for modernising the current framework in order to deliver public service media (PSM) for audiences watching broadcast TV and online."

All political parties are committed to the general meaning of "levelling up".

In that context, this piece is about local journalism, local culture, levelling up and the need for more money, not less, for public service

---

[1] "With or without me, Florida will always be wonderfully, unrelentingly weird" by Carl Hiaasen, Miami Herald, March 12 2021.

media. Independent local journalism needs to be robust enough to call out corruption when it finds it. Levelling up should include funding autonomous geographical media centres of editorial influence and budgetary power.

'Jobsworth'

What do I mean by "jobsworth"?

"An official who upholds petty rules even at the expense of humanity or common sense."[1]

Ofcom's rules are not so petty but the organisation has never excelled at humanity or common sense. On my current usual beat, ethnic diversity, *Ofcom* ignores the issue of racism in broadcasters.[2] It turns a blind eye to pain, humanity and defies common sense.

Ofcom limits its view of "public service media (PSM)" to "audiences watching broadcast TV and online." It appears to see PSM as predominantly Public Service Broadcasters with added digital. This is both simplistic and misguided. The concept of Public Service Media should be extended beyond this narrow, backwards-looking characterisation. Public Service Media must be defined by a purpose, not by a business model or a distribution model. The definition should instead embrace a wide range of content platforms and suppliers. Equality and fairness should be an underlying principle in the allocation of public funds, not just for under-represented groups but also for under-represented localities too.

There was and still is, albeit to an ever-diminishing degree, some regional media beyond the world of the public service broadcasters.

The sustainable future for journalism was considered in detail by *The Cairncross Review* in its report of February 2019.

Less punchy than Hiaasen, Cairncross said it is: "at the local and regional level that the provision of public-interest news is most threatened. Collapsing revenue hasn't just led to cut-backs; it has cut a swathe through the local press" and "there is an immediate need to

---

[1] Oxford Languages def via Google.

[2] "Ofcom's blind eye to racism must end" 27.02.2021
https://cbesite.wordpress.com/2021/01/27/ofcoms-blind-eye-to-racism-must-end/.

plug gaps at the local level, to ensure public institutions are sufficiently held to account."

To treat the term Public Service Media as though it solely refers to public service broadcasters who also have digital content, completely ignores the findings of the *Cairncross Review* and the many manifestations of public interest news. It makes no sense. *Ofcom's* limited interpretation of the term Public Service Media stems from a jobsworth observance of its statutory constraints.

The government should end this fragmented approach. Funds should be targeted at funding autonomous geographical centres of editorial influence and budgetary power, informed by the communities in which they are based. It should provide an effective mechanism for achieving "levelling up" – not only for local journalism but for local culture as well.

Employment, economic and cultural stimulus should be spread more equitably across the Nations and Regions.

'Granada-land'

I know what an autonomous geographical centre of editorial influence and budgetary power, informed by the communities in which it was based, looks like, feels like and most important where its focus lies. My first job was with Granada TV's *World in Action* in 1969 and I then worked for Granada for 15 years from 1974- 1989.

Granada, for all its notable national and international successes, was primarily focussed on Greater Manchester, Lancashire, Merseyside, Cheshire, and Cumbria. The vast majority of the staff was home grown local talent. Only a small minority were looking towards London W1A or London W12.

As well as its main studios in Manchester, Granada had satellite offices in Liverpool, Chester and Blackburn. It nurtured North West writers like Tony Warren, Paul Abbot, Jimmy McGovern and Caroline Ahern. Home grown staff were encouraged to advance across genres. Secretaries became production assistants, some technical staff became researchers, others became camera operators. Legendary, Southport born, *World In Action* and *7 Up* cameraman, George Jesse Turner, would shoot regional documentaries with equal enthusiasm.

Granada's evening magazine programme *Granada Reports* gave first television broadcasts to the Beatles and other Merseybeat groups, as well as the Hollies. Tony Wilson on *So It Goes* gave first opportunities to numerous Manchester bands, like Happy Mondays, Joy Division and New Order.

Like many of the staff, Wilson was allowed to work across genres. As well as music, he could front the news magazine and present heavyweight multi-participant studio current affairs show. He was allowed to be an outspoken supporter of regionalism and start a campaign for North West England to be allowed a referendum on the creation of a regional assembly.

There was little freelancing, apart from the small London office. As a consequence, people were committed to the company and the region. Many jobs were internal appointments so that it was staff already committed to the region who were promoted.[1]

Sidney Bernstein, the founder, explained his huge enthusiasm for the region:

"the North is a closely knit, indigenous, industrial society; a homogeneous cultural group with a good record for music, theatre, literature and newspapers, not found elsewhere in this island, except perhaps in Scotland. Compare this with London and its suburbs—full of displaced persons. And, of course, if you look at a map of the concentration of population in the North and a rainfall map, you will see that the North is an ideal place for television".[2]

Displaced persons not the way forward

The last decade of broadcasting devolution has relied too much on displaced persons, staff moved from London, rather than home grown local talent. Public service media needs to be funded to achieve the development of greater plurality and more locally focussed media with home grown workers. It happened before, it can happen again.

The latest BBC plans for devolution are, in many respects, to be welcomed, moving additional funds to existing centres in Belfast,

---

[1] From a note by Dr Stephen Kelly, Project Director Granadaland oral history, Granadaland.com

[2] Pearson, Tony. "Bernstein, Sidney". Museum of Broadcast Communications.

Birmingham, Bristol, Cardiff, Glasgow and Salford. But 600 news posts will be made redundant and none of the top executives will be moving out of London. Former BBC Editorial Director, Roger Mosey has written:

"Look at the detail, though, and doubts multiply. For a start, not a single member of the Executive Board will be moving; and nor will anyone from the BBC News board. In exchanges with staff, both Davie and his Director of News Fran Unsworth have been challenged about why they are not packing their bags – but more bothering is that none of their senior colleagues are either."[1]

Mosey (a former Editor of *'Today'*) concludes: " It doesn't go far enough to proclaim now that the *Today* programme and News*night* will be presented on location more often. This is journalism via an overnight stay in the Travelodge, not a deep-rooted commitment to a region in which you live and work and educate the kids."

Announcements over the past year, have shown an increasing concentration of editorial power in the new role of BBC Content Officer, currently held by Charlotte Moore. The BBC continues to move to a less pluralistic approach. All pyramids are subsumed within in the Content Officer's giant pyramid. Eyes are ever more focused on the power concentrated in W1A.

The regional ITV system was better designed to sustain and promote regional diversity and, yes, to "level up", even though that term was decades from invention.

The ITV system was based on an economic model that couldn't last. Now the time has come to reinvent the wheel with a new model. Greater funding for public service media will be needed.

More Money, Not Less

The debate about funding public service media has been closely linked to a debate about funding the BBC. Such a narrow focus is likely to lead to a reduction in public funding for public service media.

---

[1] "Tim Davie's BBC 'transformation' doesn't go far enough" by Roger Mosey, The Spectator, 22 March 2021.

The case for increased funding for public service media, with wider scope, wider distribution and better targeting should be considered even if it currently extends beyond *Ofcom's* remit.

There is a lack of fresh thinking and new ideas. The best brains are either employed by the broadcasters who are focussed on medium term survival or *Ofcom* which pursues too narrow a path. In the interest of media plurality and levelling up, the BBC (with *S4C*) should no longer be the exclusive arbiter on the distribution of public funding for public service media.

How public service media should be funded is beyond my scope. There are now a range of viable complementary or alternative models to the licence fee.

This is not about top slicing BBC funding. This is about extending the vision for public service media and increasing the funding. A vision that extends beyond worried broadcasters and faltering regional newspapers to set an environment where new institutions and delivery systems can be born and flourish alongside the legacy media.

The BBC says new research from KPMG shows the BBC has "wide ranging economic impacts on the UK economy" and makes "a significant economic contribution across each of the UK's nations and regions." In the interest of levelling up, why stop at the BBC?

Levelling Up

From where I sit, *Ofcom* looks like a general hospital with superb geriatric care but no midwives to encourage new births.

Some say I am wrong to attack *Ofcom* for merely working within the limits it has been given and that I am allowing my frustrations with *Ofcom's* inadequate response to diversity issues to cloud my judgement on where *Ofcom*'s boundaries should lie. They say I should look to the government.

This government has, in John Whittingdale, a minister with deeper and longer knowledge of broadcasting and media issues than any of his predecessors from any party.

When the government comes to focus on the longer-term issues of levelling up, perhaps Whittingdale will develop a vision which sees funding autonomous geographical media centres of editorial influence and budgetary power as one of the effective mechanisms for achieving "levelling up".

As it stands, I fear *Ofcom's* current jobsworth approach will rule out the possibility of it advocating for a wider range of public service media with increased funding to support local, autonomous media with budgets and power.

About the Contributor

Simon Albury was formerly CEO of the Royal Television Society and Chair of the Centre for Investigative Journalism and is currently Chair of the Campaign for Broadcasting Equality.

Chapter Nine

Just what does *Ofcom* mean by Diversity?

> Marcus Ryder established the Sir Lenny Henry Centre for Media Diversity in 2020 to address what he saw as a deficit in UK media taking a more academic and systematic approach to tackling diversity issues. Here he argues economic theories of market failure should dictate *Ofcom*'s actions.

What is the point of *Ofcom*?

This is not a rhetorical question but one we should keep at the forefront of our minds when we are discussing diversity in the UK media industry.

First of all, *Ofcom* is the "government-approved regulatory and competition authority for the broadcasting, telecommunications and postal industries of the United Kingdom". Its job is not to try and make people "nicer" or to make sure people are "kinder" to each other.

It is a market regulator in the same way *Ofwat* (Water Services Regulation Authority) regulates the water industry or *Ofgem* (Office of Gas and Electricity Markets) regulates the UK's gas and electricity networks. Sometimes because television is a creative industry, full of creative artistic people we seem to forget this cold reality. The regulators are there to address market failures which left to their own devices would disadvantage the UK population.

Market not personal failure

This is how we must see the television industry's lack of diversity. We must see it as a market failure. Too often when we discuss media diversity we frame it in terms of the personal failings of a few executives or commissioners. For example, I frequently hear people saying if we could only increase the diversity of the gatekeepers we could solve diversity. For me this is akin to saying that if we could only get nice liberal people to run our energy companies we would not have to worry about regulating them properly.

If the lack of diversity is a market failure and *Ofcom*'s job is to address market failures, then the first thing we need to acknowledge, however hard, is that *Ofcom* has failed the television industry so far when it comes to diversity. Statistics suggest that diversity in the industry has barely kept pace with the demographic changes of the UK, and in some areas has even gone backwards.

Why? And is it really *Ofcom's* fault? One way to understand how *Ofcom* currently regulates television diversity versus how it should is to examine other (accepted) market failures in the television industry and how *Ofcom* addresses these.

Tv is full of market failures-how to solve them

The television industry is actually full of market failures. For instance, television broadcasters left to their own devices will not produce enough quality news and current affairs programmes, favouring entertainment programmes instead with larger audiences and more revenue.

Unregulated, broadcasters will not produce enough high-quality children's programmes as certain types of advertising targeting them is prohibited and it is a small audience nationally, so it doesn't make "market" sense to target them. Another example is the production of programmes outside of London, it often makes "market" sense to have all producers in the same place.

To solve these types of market failures the regulator has to step in and actually shape the market setting quotas and issuing license requirements. Specifically for all the above examples, *Ofcom* insists that broadcasters produce a set quota of news and current affairs programmes, Children's programmes and programmes outside of London.

Importantly what *Ofcom* does *not* do is insist that producers of Children's programmes receive more training in the hope that they will be able to compete with cheaper light entertainment programmes.

Ofcom also does not produce reports on the lack of Out of London or Children's programmes arguing that "sunlight is the best disinfectant" and more information will help broadcasters realise the error of their ways and commission more programmes.

Last but not least, *Ofcom* does not ask broadcasters to implement "unconscious bias training" for senior managers to commission more Welsh or Scottish programmes - as if somehow the lack of out of London programmes is due to some inbuilt prejudice.

Will these 'solutions' work for *Ofcom*?

Now I mention all these "solutions" in a slightly tongue-in-cheek manner, but I have a serious point. These are all solutions that I have heard *Ofcom* as a body, or individual members of *Ofcom*, support explicitly or implicitly when trying to address television's lack of diversity.

But they are not the right – nor usual – set of solutions for a regulator to focus on. When it comes to addressing genre and regional diversity the regulator has realised that it needs to focus on the market failures inherent in how the industry operates, not on the individuals working in the market. No number of *Ofcom* diversity reports or diversity schemes will solve the problem of low numbers of Black Asian and Minority Ethnic (BAME), disabled people and women in the industry.

So why hasn't this happened so far, specifically for diversity, while it has happened for the other market failures in the industry? The problem with the lack of diversity market failure is that there is an even bigger market failure that lies behind it, which *Ofcom* has yet to acknowledge, at least in public as being the core reason for the lack of diversity-that the UK television industry effectively being a "monopsony".

What is a "monopsony" you ask?

Well, most people have heard of a monopoly – and no I don't mean the board game! A monopoly – as a concept – is when you have a large number of *buyers* of a certain product or service but only one *seller* of the product or service.

The real examples of monopoly that most people come across are railway companies or electricity companies. A few companies can dictate how much people pay for the product, provide a bad service and have other negative effects for the consumer, but still increase their profits. The negatives of monopolies are well-known and governments often have to intervene to try and either break them up or legislate against their worst actions. Indeed, the kinds of regulators

I mentioned right at the beginning of this piece – the *Ofwats* and the *Ofgems* – are often created to regulate these "monopolistic" industries.

A monopsony has similarly negative consequences but it is like a monopoly in reverse. A monopsony is when you have lots of *sellers* of a product but only one *buyer*. In these circumstances it is the buyers who can dictate the price and how the market works. It is a classic case of market failure.

And increasingly that is precisely what many economists think we have in the television industry. Strictly speaking it is an oligopsony – as they are just a few buyers in this market, but let's keep it simple for now.

The fact is, most freelancers and independent companies might not have heard of monopsony theory but whenever I talk to friends in the industry they quickly recognize the situation of competing with hundreds of other companies (sellers) but only having a handful of broadcasters (buyers) they can pitch their ideas to whom to sell their programmes.

Increasingly monopsony theory is being used by economists to explain why diversity problems exists in various industries. It is no coincidence that both the tech and television industries seem to suffer from a lack of diversity and both have the problem of a few large companies dominating their industries.

Economics at bed time?

Now I love economics – I studied economics at university, I am currently a financial journalist, and I am married to one of the leading economists in China-Africa relations. Just the other day I was talking to her about Neo-paleo-Keynesian Phillips Curves. And bedroom pillow talk can sometimes stray into subjects such as Friedrich List's theories on infant industry protection. But I realise other people might not similarly love the dismal science so here's the warning; as L'Oreal used to say - concentrate because here comes the science bit:

Monopsony theory goes a long way to explaining the entrenched diversity problems in the UK TV and film industry, such as only 3 percent of people working behind the camera in the film industry being from a BAME background or that number falling to 0.3 percent when it comes to disabled people.

Two sides of the same coin?

While there will always be competition for the very best talent, say the top one percent, the vast majority of us are somewhere in the middle. What monopsony theory tells us is that while the companies might fight over a very few people (actually inflating their wages) there is less competition by companies to battle it out for the other workers. Monopsony theory can explain why broadcasters will fight over the talents of Steve McQueen and Micheala Cole while the rest of the industry can remain remarkably un-diverse.

These two things are not contradictory; they are in fact two sides of the same coin. The market failures associated with monopsonies mean that companies will more likely hire their friends, promote people that look like them and retain people that they like rather than people who might be the best person for the job. In a free market if you did this you would quickly be punished.

In a monopsony (or oligopsony) you will hardly feel the consequences of your actions - at least in the short to medium-term. So what does this mean for those of us who want to increase diversity in the film and television industry? Should we all just give up because we are working in a monopsony?

No! We definitely should not give up

But monopsony theory does teach us that we need to look at different types of solutions as opposed to the usual ones people in the industry often mention. It also teaches us that it is unrealistic to think market participants (the broadcasters) can solve market failures irrespective of their best intentions. It would literally go against all conventional economic theory – and their fundamental interests as ologopsonists (!) - to do so.

It must be up to the regulator.

Dealing with monopoly – and in this case monopsony is precisely what regulators like *Ofcom* exist to do. *Ofcom* should not be, and is normally not about trying to get individual people to act better. Yet this is how it has been with regards to diversity so far.

Ofcom is an industry regulator established to address market failures.

The lack of diversity is a market failure. As a result, there is only one way the lack of diversity will be solved. Regulation. In this respect, all roads lead to *Ofcom,* doing what it does for other market failures. I look forward to it taking up this crucial role.

About the Contributor

Marcus Ryder is a Visiting Professor of Media Diversity at Birmingham City University. He worked at the BBC for 24 years, the last eight as head of current affairs at BBC Scotland. He attributes his experience of the corporation's attempts at increasing out of London diversity as shaping his views on increasing other forms of diversity.

Chapter Ten

Ofcom: a *Naked Attraction* to liberals?

Ofcom **says it is not a censor but it has the power to silence broadcasters if they break its rules.** *Ofcom's* **judgements are political. It is a mechanism for controlling public debate in the UK and should be clearly understood as such.**
Robin Aitken discusses.

Kevin Bakhurst, *Ofcom's* group director of content and media policy wrote this on its website in 2020: "We never censor content. Our powers to sanction broadcasters who breach our rules apply only after a programme has aired. In fact, the clear, fair and respected code that we enforce on TV and radio acts as a strong deterrent against poor behaviour. Secondly, we are independent from Government, free from corporate or political influence."

This invites a discussion about what the word 'censor' actually means. It is true that *Ofcom* does not conform to the stereotype of the official censor, blue pencil in hand, striking out innuendo and smutty jokes. Nevertheless it is an undeniable fact that *Ofcom's* rules – officially known as '*The Ofcom Broadcasting Code*' is a compendium of do's and don'ts which broadcasters must obey on pain of losing their licence. And when you delve into the code's contents many of its provisions seem to circumscribe what broadcasters can say. To anyone, familiar with America's full-blooded First amendment constitutional guarantee of the right to free-speech, *Ofcom's* code might seem very much like a censor's charter.

The comparison with the US might seem like a mere debating point, because this is the UK and we have our own rules, but it points to an essential truth about *Ofcom's* role which is that it is part of the mechanism by which allowable discourse in Britain is policed. The *Ofcom* code is a useful guide to understanding the 'Overton Window'[1] within which public debate in Britain is conducted. And I argue that –

---

[1] The Overton Window, also known as the 'window of discourse' is a concept devised by policy analyst Joseph Overton which describes the range of policies acceptable for public debate.

despite its protestations to the contrary, *Ofcom* is very much in the business of controlling that debate. Whether one calls that 'censorship' or not is a semantic argument but there is no doubt that *Ofcom* uses its powers to banish from the airwaves viewpoints and ideas it does not like.

Banning 'hate speech'

On January 1 2021 the organisation issued an updated version of the code and eyebrows were raised about the way that one section – on so-called 'hate-speech' - had been enlarged. The previous version forbade broadcasters from airing anything which incited hate on just four grounds: race, sex, religion and nationality; the new version lists fourteen categories that *Ofcom* now views as protected characteristics: disability, ethnicity, social origin, gender, sex, gender reassignment, nationality, race, religion or belief, colour, genetic features, language, political or any other opinion.

This list is very much in accord with the spirit of the times whereby there is an ever-expanding catalogue of characteristics which the law seeks to protect; *Ofcom's* new code merely reflects the view, which now predominates in legal and political circles, that free-speech cannot be allowed if it is at the expense of giving offence or hurting someone's feelings. Though it nowhere says so explicitly the code draws its justification from the idea that certain ideas, certain words, certain viewpoints pose a danger to society and therefore broadcasters should not engage with them.

As an example, consider what happened at the beginning of the Covid-19 pandemic in 2020. Though there was widespread support for the public health measures introduced at the time, acceptance was not universal; there were dissenters who questioned the validity of the measures – face masks, social distancing, lock-down etc - and some who even doubted the reality of a global viral pandemic. *Ofcom*, at government prompting, issued guidance notes for broadcasters warning them not to air material which might undermine official advice.

Subsequently, *Ofcom* ruled against six broadcasters which in its view had broken the rules; in one instance a radio station had broadcast an 80-minute interview with David Icke allowing him to expound his 'theory' that the whole coronavirus pandemic was a ruse by a New World Order to impose its will. Angered by what it saw as an attempt to improperly restrict free debate, The Free Speech Union[1] sought judicial review against *Ofcom's* guidance notes , arguing that it had overstepped its remit. They lost the case.

You might feel that little is lost by preventing Mr Icke giving us the benefit of his idiosyncratic beliefs – but should he be banned from airing them? It is questions like this that go to the heart of the debate about *Ofcom's* role. It is quite easy to mount a justification of the pandemic guidance note based on the notion of the 'common good': it can be reasoned that the virus posed a serious risk to public health and it was in everyone's interests that sober, evidence-based, public health rules should not be undermined by crackpot conspiracy theorists. Therefore, we might conclude, *Ofcom* did us all a favour – but there is no denying the fact, in my view, that in doing so Mr Icke's, and others', rights to 'free-speech' were compromised.

Watchdog with teeth?

In these decisions it is all a question of judgement – and it is *Ofcom's* judgement which deserves scrutiny. Because it has real teeth, including the ultimate sanction of withdrawing a broadcast licence, broadcasters are easily brought back into the Overton fold. But whereas it acts swiftly to silence broadcasters on some issues it has often shown a marked reluctance to rein in broadcasters who have aggressively promoted permissive liberal values.

An interesting example of this is the Channel 4 show *Naked Attraction*, now in its seventh series. It is a dating show where young people strip naked, examine each other's genitals and then make a choice about whether or not to date. When first shown in 2016 there were many complaints from people who objected to what they saw as cheap and exploitative televisual voyeurism.

The objectors might have saved their breath; *Ofcom* decided that *Naked Attraction* was just fine. It broke none of their rules and in the watchdog's view was merely a new twist on a dating show and there was no sexual activity as such. Also, they said, it was allowed because it went out after the so-called 'watershed' (that is later in the evening when it is supposed young children will not be watching – a concept which time-shift services have rendered entirely obsolete).

---

[1] The Free Speech Union was founded in 2020 by the journalist Toby Young. It campaigns to preserve free speech

Is *Naked Attraction* for the Common Good?

The question arises whether in the case of *Naked Attraction* it is possible to apply the same 'common good' arguments as were deployed in the guidance note on pandemic coverage. What are the societal benefits of the programme and what its harms? From a socially conservative point of view there are no benefits but only dis-benefits: such a programme sexually objectifies both women and men, it encourages sexual promiscuity and treats sex as a mere entertainment, it makes public something which should properly be private and it exploits the human sex-drive for ratings success.

I think it is degenerate and debasing. But *Ofcom* took a different view and found no reason not to allow the programme to air. To any social conservative that suggests that their rulings are informed by a different, permissive set of standards.

Moreover, the stance that *Ofcom* took on *Naked Attraction* seems at odds with parts of its own code part of which is specifically entitled 'Protecting the Under 18s'. According to that, broadcasters should not publish material that 'might impair the physical, mental or moral development of under 18s'. How, given that *Naked Attraction*, is available on catch-up and thus available to all, can that ruling be squared with its own rules? The strong suspicion is that *Ofcom* merely enforces the code according to its own favoured 'media morality' which has binned the old rules of moral behaviour in favour of an easy-going permissiveness.

The rules by which society decides what is(and what is not) acceptable change over time and we should not get hung-up on the example of one programme like *Naked Attraction*; indeed the only point of mentioning it is to draw a contrast with the way *Ofcom* decided on how to limit the debate about the pandemic. In one instance it was permissive, in the other restrictive but – and this is the crucial point – in both cases they made a judgement and that judgement is the collective opinion of *Ofcom's* 'Content Board' – the internal committee which adjudicates on individual programmes and broadcasters. By virtue of their membership of the board this panel of media-savvy individuals are empowered to transmit into the public sphere their own prejudices and predilections and experience.

Who decides the direction of *Ofcom*?

Which brings us to the current question of who should sit on the 'Content Board'. At the time of writing the post of chair of *Ofcom* is vacant and it has been strongly rumoured that the ex-editor of *The Daily Mail*, Paul Dacre, a noted social conservative, is in the running for the job. This has caused an outcry in some quarters – mainly from social liberals who fear that were he to be appointed *Ofcom* might begin to chart a different course. It is plain common sense that it matters who gets to make these decisions; if the Content Board is stacked with permissive liberals you will get one sort of ruling, were it to be composed of social conservatives there would be different rulings.

I think there can be little doubt that since its formation – in 2003 – *Ofcom* has 'dressed left'; its ruling have ultimately favoured a liberal-left view of the world and this has suited the broadcasters very well. The BBC, for instance, has had very little trouble from *Ofcom* since 2017 when it was granted oversight on their PSB content.

This is unsurprising as many of *Ofcom*'s senior executives are ex-BBC editorial figures, including the aforementioned Kevin Bakhurst, *Ofcom* Content and Policy Director who was Controller of the BBC's 24 hour News in a previous incarnation. The BBC is, itself, a socially liberal organisation whose world-view inclines towards the progressive left[1] and there is a strong suspicion on the socially conservative Right that the two organisations share a common outlook.

Appointing someone like Paul Dacre would be a statement of intent by the Johnson government that it does not intend that this state of affairs should be permanent and that it wants the balance redressed. Were that to happen it would signal, perhaps, that the political pendulum was again in motion, this time moving towards the socially conservative Right. The liberal-Left should not be surprised by such a development; they have 'owned the game' in broadcasting for the past 50 years and a correction is overdue.

---

[1] For a full discussion of this point see the author's book *The Noble Liar* (Biteback Publishing 2020).

About the Contributor

Robin Aitken was a BBC reporter for 25 years, latterly on *The Today Programme*. Since leaving the BBC he has published several books about the Corporation. He regularly writes on media matters for *The Daily Telegraph, The Spectator* and other newspapers and magazines. He lives in Oxford where he founded the Oxford Food Bank, for which he was awarded an MBE.

Section Two
Taming The Tiger? Regulating The BBC

John Mair

It was like a sardine swallowing a whale when *Ofcom* took on regulation of all the BBC Public Service content from 2017. It was fiercely resisted in embryo by the then Director General Mark Thompson when first proposed and, as Bill Emmott pointed out in an earlier essay in this book, the early days of *Ofcom* BBC regulation were very rocky on the Content side.

Jacquie Hughes was poached from a role in the BBC as a producer to head up the new BBC regulation at *Ofcom* in 2016-2020. In **'Notes from the Frontline'**, she sets out her stall very well in terms of the promises of performance and sanctions which *Ofcom* forced the BBC to undertake.

So far, the Corporation has had, by and large, a clean bill of health from the regulator. Mild slaps here and there - on 'yoof' inter alia - but no huge rows-yet.

Peter Jukes runs an alternative left-wing website, *Byline Times*. He is a long-term critic of the MSM - Main Stream Media - especially the right-wing press in the UK. He sat through the entire Old Bailey phone hacking trials tweeting every day to 'enlighten' people and wrote a book '*Beyond Contempt: The Inside Story of the Phone Hacking Trial*' thereafter.

Jukes is a long-term fan of the BBC and its seeming neutrality, but he sees it being in big peril: from the outside by the Tory Brexit right who see it as 'woke' and 'culturally Marxist', and from the inside by what he sees as its cravenness in imposing 'due impartiality' on its output. He argues this has legitimised extremist views and, still to come, the granting of new licences to 'News with views' (Andrew Neil's GB News and the Murdoch lookalike). Jukes looks to *Ofcom* to hold the ring on impartiality but is in despair should the Johnson favourite Paul Dacre, scourge of the liberal elite, get the job. In his words **'the BBC and Broadcast Journalism is the Frontline of a Culture War'**.

Chapter Eleven

Regulating the BBC: Notes from the front-line

Jacquie Hughes was a BBC Producer and Executive until she jumped over the fence to join Ofcom to regulate her former employer. What did she learn on the other side?

Given the level of scrutiny *Ofcom* receives for its regulation of the BBC, it is easy to forget it has a huge slate of other responsibilities - including oversight of the nation's telecommunications infrastructure - and that it has only had full oversight of the BBC's for the last 5 years.

Yet political and public interest in the regulator tends to focus exclusively on its relationship to the BBC. Would there be such intense interest in who is the new Chair of *Ofcom* if it hadn't been given oversight of the BBC?

Everyone inside and outside *Ofcom* knew that if the government moved regulation of the BBC from the BBC Trust to *Ofcom*, that the regulator's other work would fade into the shadows and all eyes would turn to its handling of this much loved and much studied British institution.

Every move would be poured over by politicians, other media players, the public and media academics: would *Ofcom* get 'captured' by the BBC and its powerful allies? Would it stray into BBC governance issues? Would *Ofcom* ever truly understand the unique market position of the BBC, given its essential function to date was as an economic regulator?

And so, it came to pass. The BBC is, after all, a bit like the nation's Christmas tree; everyone wants it to shine for them, to hang their particular interest 'bauble' on it, or expect it to host a present just for them; some think it is overdressed and crowds out the rest, others are convinced it is not as sparkly as it used to be.

Entering the Lion's den

I know this from first-hand experience; I was appointed Director of Content Policy by *Ofcom* in 2016 and charged with developing an approach to overseeing BBC performance and creating a new Operating Licence for the Corporation. *Ofcom* had recognised it needed more people with a deep understanding of public service broadcasting, and the BBC*'s* unique status as an intervention in the market, and brought onside some new hires with this background.

I'd been a programme maker and Commissioner at the BBC, worked at the BBC Trust, and been an academic with research and publications focused on the role regulation plays in securing the public interest and purposes of public service broadcasting. I'd written about accountability and the key difference between regulation and governance.

As an Advisor to the House of Lords Communications Select Committee during the Charter review period, I'd supported its conclusion that an independent regulator holding the BBC to account through a clearer, simplified framework was a good idea. We said the new regulator should conduct a 'root and branch review of its accountability framework', to clarify and simplify it.

I'd previously expressed doubts abou*t Ofcom* being given the whole of the regulation of the BBC, given its primary function to was to 'uphold' the market, but I was mainly worried that giving it more regulatory powers did not 'fix' the governance issues of the BBC. The BBC is a public institution, public interest rests in the institution and its governing body should be demonstrably independent and itself accountable for its responsibilities.

In a paper for think tank CentreForum: *'Broadcasting by Consent: the* BBC, *Public Service Broadcasting and Charter Renewal in 2017'*, I concluded that *Ofcom* would be the best adjudicator of the efficiency, effectiveness and appropriateness of PSB and the role of the BBC in delivering it, but that governance needed to sit with an independent body. The BBC Trust had held this role; it now passed to a new Executive Board within the BBC, made up of internal and external members.

Governance is NOT regulation

It was vital that *Ofcom* set out - and others understood - the clear distinction between governance and regulation. The new arrangement confirmed *Ofcom* would not be a 'Shadow Board'. Under the new 2016 Charter, the BBC Board and *Ofcom* have distinct roles. The Board must ensure the BBC acts in the public interest and meets its wider Charter obligations and oversee strategy, service delivery, efficiency and performance measurement in the first interest. *Ofcom's* role is to act where the BBC isn't delivering for audiences and ensure it acts reasonably concerning others in the sector. The Charter also reconfirmed that the Government of the day must respect the BBC's editorial and operational independence.

Despite the separation of roles, it became clear that everyone with an interest in the BBC would make a beeline to *Ofcom* to share it and expect *Ofcom* to take up its particular cause. Understandably, given access to the BBC to discuss what it did and how it did it had been hitherto virtually impossible; its ways of working described to us as a 'black box'. *Ofcom* encouraged this, by making clear it would ensure the views of citizens, consumers and stakeholders would feed into and shape our 'BBC thinking'.

2016 BBC Charter: A clean break

The 2016 Charter and Agreement was the biggest reform of the BBC's governance and regulation arrangements since it was founded nine decades before: a clean break with the old regime. In handing responsibility for regulation for the first time to an external body the government signalled its intention for the BBC to be more robustly held to account for its standards, potential impact on the market, overall performance and independence.

Trusting *Ofcom* with this new function was recognition of the regulator's track record, scale, credibility and existing role in certain key areas of PSB delivery – and the value of its overview of the whole sector at a time of increasing convergence and interconnectedness. *Ofcom* is, by necessity, independent of the government and the organisations it regulates. The BBC is explicitly allowed to take creative risks and choose how it organises itself – provided it continues to comply with its over-arching duties. The regulator should not get involved in the minutiae of its creative decision-making processes, scheduling decisions or management structures.

We made this clear in our statement in early 2017 of the overall approach to regulating the BBC to:

Recognise that the BBC *is the cornerstone of broadcasting*

Firmly place initial responsibility with the new BBC *Board*

Make good use of our depth of knowledge and experience

Ensure stakeholders are consulted

Provide clarity about our expectations of the BBC

Ofcom already had some duties concerning editorial complaints - holding the BBC to account under the rules of its Broadcasting Code, and competition – conducting Market Impact Assessments (MIA's) for new or changing services, but responsibility for BBC performance was a new and high priority task. This was the area I stepped into, to develop an approach to accountability for performance, across services.

We had set out our stall:

- to set enforceable regulatory conditions; the BBC would face sanctions, including – for the first time – the possibility of financial penalties if it failed to meet these regulatory conditions
- to assess compliance with these through a new performance measurement framework
- to report annually on these performance measures and the BBC's compliance
- to conduct at least two in-depth reviews of the BBC's performance, and conduct ad hoc reviews, where we felt appropriate

We proposed setting a single Licence for all the BBC's UK public services, replacing the existing system of individual service licenses, and allowing it to be adapted in the future. The new Licence came into force in January 2018. It placed tougher requirements on the BBC than before and set it over 150 licence conditions.

The BBC has met all of its licence conditions every year, but *Ofcom* has urged it to go further in terms of serving younger audiences, to respond more urgently to audiences' habits and changing markets, to improve the way it engages with the public on its plans, to be more proactive in engaging with others in the industry on its plans, and more transparent about its investment, strategy and performance in the nations and regions. It has repeatedly urged the BBC Board to take the lead.

Has *Ofcom* regulation worked on the BBC?

There is no question that the BBC is better held to account by *Ofcom* than by previous arrangements. *Ofcom's* existing experience in upholding broadcast standards and in assessing competition stood it in good stead for absorbing responsibility for the BBC.

In respect of its responsibility for BBC performance, certain aspects such as setting numerical quotas for certain genre and channels were straightforward, and *Ofcom's* approach has been thorough, visible, accountable. For the less quantifiable aspects; 'high quality', 'distinctiveness', 'authenticity', *Ofcom* has been challenged – as all other agents throughout history - to try and measure the less easily measurable.

Returning to my opening statement; everyone expects the BBC to work for them; to reflect their interests - after all the BBC has baked-in commitment to 'reflect, represent and serve the diverse communities of all of the United Kingdom's nations and regions and, in doing so, support the creative economy across the United Kingdom', to quote Public Purpose Four of its licence. That goes further, requiring the BBC to 'accurately represent and authentically portray the diverse communities of the whole of the United Kingdom'.

'Representation' means the extent to which people and characters appear. *Ofcom* expects the number of people appearing in BBC programmes to broadly reflect the population of the United Kingdom. 'Portrayal' means how these people and characters are depicted and here, qualitative analysis is needed here to ask if people feel it is authentic.

This proved to be the hottest topic of debate and source of petitioning at the time of writing the Licence and remains the performance indicator *Ofcom* is still least satisfied with in the third annual report published in November 2020.

The BBC uses a measurement proxy for audience satisfaction ('effectiveness'). *Ofcom* thinks this is too narrow and has asked the BBC to consider 'a more holistic range of measures' and set out the steps it will take to improve audiences' perceptions.

It's an almost impossible conundrum: when we watch the BBC, should we expect to see ourselves perfectly reflected, in all our multiple aspects: sex, age, geography, ethnicity, religion, social status? Or should we view it as a window, in which we look to see examples of difference? Or can we expect both? And how can that aspiration be achieved?

While *Ofcom's* regulation of the BBC is regarded as a success, unsettled and I expect this one topic will still be debated and unsettled - and feature in every *Ofcom* annual reports of BBC performance for many a year to come.

About the Contributor.

Jacquie Hughes was *Ofcom* Director of Content Policy, with responsibility for BBC performance, from 2016-2020. Previously she had been a BBC/ITV producer and a university lecturer.

Chapter Twelve

Why the BBC and Broadcast Journalism is the Frontline of a Culture War

With the appointment of a former Conservative Candidate as Director-General of the BBC, and a major Conservative donor as its chair, Peter Jukes of Byline Times *wonders if the BBC is being consumed from within.*

In the ten years since I first started covering the phone-hacking scandal at the News of the World, and the connection between the dark arts of Fleet Street and the murder of private detective Daniel Morgan, one of the few consolations of immersing myself in what former Prime Minister Gordon Brown called the "criminal-media nexus" was the realisation that Britain's broadcasters provided an antidote to our hyper-partisan press.

However partial or self-serving the coverage of Britain's newspapers, dominated by Conservative thinkers and owned by millionaires, often based overseas, most of the public consumed their news from TV and Radio, and though the press often set the agenda both in terms of rhetoric and breaking new stories, the country mainly saw itself through the prism of public service principles of impartiality, fairness and accuracy. It might be staid and a bit boring, but it was safe.

Compare that to the US in the last 30 years. Ever since President Ronald Reagan dropped the Fairness Doctrine (and made Rupert Murdoch a US citizen) its broadcast environment, driven by outlets like Fox News, has become more polemical and attuned to heat and argument rather than illumination and fact. This anger and disinformation culminated in the denial of the 2020 election results. Shock-jock commentary and baseless conspiracy theory was a key factor in the attack on the US Capitol on 6 January this year, which left 5 people dead and shook American democracy as profoundly as any event since 9/11 (See Mark Thompson Chapter 4 and Clive Myrie Chapter 4 in this volume).

Those events will reverberate for years in the US. Fox News, and even more extreme new competitors such as OAN and Newsmax now face billion-dollar legal challenges from the electoral machine voting counting company Dominion Voting Systems because of the various conspiracy theories they pumped out over months regarding voter fraud.[1]

Rather than learn the lessons of the US, and the danger to democracy of a fact-free broadcast regime based on hyperventilating opinions, the UK seems to be following down the same dark path, and without a stable or reliable print journalism regime (as the US still has) to counter it.

Fox in the Coop

It's too early to say whether the news outlet *GB News* will be a step down that rocky road, but the early signs aren't good. Though clothed in the flag of patriotism, key executives and financiers of the news channel are actually based overseas, bringing the same problems of accountability we've witnessed for years with Rupert Murdoch and other newspaper proprietors who are 'non-domiciled' overseas for tax purposes.

The apparent agenda of *GB News* main figurehead, former *Sunday Times* editor and BBC presenter Andrew Neil, seems to be cultural warfare and challenging 'woke' opinion - i.e. the supposedly liberal hegemony over issues such as race and gender. He complained in the *Daily Express* that Britain's "national conversation has become too metropolitan, too southern and too middle-class" and opined that "some journalists and commentators seem too confident that their liberal-left assumptions must surely be shared by every sensible person in the land".[2]

---

[1] McCarthy Tom (2021), 'Dominion Voting Systems sues Fox News for $1.6bn over election fraud lies', *Guardian*, 21 March. Available at
https://www.theguardian.com/media/2021/mar/26/fox-news-sued-dominion-2020-election-voting-fraud-lies.

[2] Neil, Andrew (2021), 'UK news debate is woke and out of touch – prepare for a huge TV shake-up'. *Daily Express*, 7 February. Available at
https://www.express.co.uk/comment/expresscomment/1394315/Andrew-Neil-GB-News-latest-comment.

Though some of *GB News*'s announced hires are experienced and trusted journalists, the focus has been on political provocateurs, or pundits from the Guido Fawkes blog, the Sun and former candidates from Nigel Farage's Brexit Party. There's no pretence at objectivity, but rather -- as Fox News supremo Roger Ailes declared at its foundation - Neil is channelling a sense of grievance and rectifying what he felt was a massive bias towards 'liberals' in the media.

While *GB News* has yet to launch, and Murdoch's competing news channel from News UK is still be unveiled, the real prize in the broadcasting battle is the BBC. The public sector dwarves the new giants, like a giant dinosaur compared to some small early rodent-like animals.

And that may ultimately be the point. Dinosaurs died out and the rodent-like mammals inherited the earth.

'BBC In Peril-in the past'

I'm old enough to remember comparable moments of peril for the BBC over the second half of its hundred years of existence: the removal of Alastair Milne as Director-General after the controversy of the *Real Lives* documentary about the conflict in Northern Ireland in the 80s; the resignation of Greg Dyke in the fallout about reporting the alleged 'dodgy dossier' on Saddam Hussein's missile capabilities in the noughties. Both affected me directly as both a viewer, citizen, and a freelance writer for the BBC.

But during all those turbulent times, and the inevitable attempts by political parties to influence the nation's broadcaster, I still sensed that the structures around the BBC, the systems of governance designed to make sure it could recover from the rounds of bloodletting and palace coups, were in place. After all, ever since I was born, the BBC was a vaunted arms-length body, which somehow embodied the key values of the country (like them or loathe them) both to the nation and across the world, without being under the direct control of the state.

With all the institutional changes of the last ten years or more, I must admit I frankly have no idea if any of those guard-rails to independence still apply. The constant jockeying and lobbying around the renewal of the license fee was always an occasion for politicians to apply pressure to the public sector broadcaster. But more subtle changes have changed the ground entirely. First regulated by the BBC

Trust, and now *OfCom*, the bedrock of institutional solidity has been replaced by the shifting sands of political appointments and jobs for the boys.

Make no mistake. For many on the right of the Conservative party, the BBC is a key target in their attempt to remake Brexit Britain in their own image. In 2004, the thinktank run by Dominic Cummings, Boris Johnson's key electoral strategist for the successful (if lawbreaking) Vote Leave campaign during the stunning General Election success of 2019, declared that the BBC was "a mortal enemy" of the Conservative party in a blogpost.[1]

Though Cummings left his role as Number 10 advisor late in 2019, this tendentious and combative attitude appears to be growing in the Conservative Party. Thanks to complaints from Conservative MPs after drawing attention to a large flag and picture of the Queen visible behind Housing Secretary Robert Jenrick during an interview in March this year, BBC Breakfast presenter Naga Munchetty was forced to apologise for liking flag-sceptical tweets.[2]

There is a underlying ideology at work behind the bluster. Cummings' close colleague, former Eurosceptic MEP, Daniel Hannan (now elevated to the Lords) described the NHS as a "mistake" on Fox News that "made people iller".[3] To those on the libertarian right both the BBC and Britain's universal health system represent some kind of 'cultural Marxism' or embedded institutional socialism.

'Due Impartiality'

The BBC hasn't helped itself in this long-running assault by misunderstanding its remit and opening up a breach for hyper-

---

[1] Cummings, Dominic (2004), "'Mortal enemy': what Cummings' thinktank said about BBC', reprinted in the *Guardian*, 21 Jan 2020. Available at https://www.theguardian.com/politics/2020/jan/21/mortal-enemy-what-cummings-thinktank-said-about-bbc.

[2] Edmonds, Lizzie (2021) 'Naga Munchetty apologises for liking 'offensive' tweet about union flag backdrop', *Evening Standard*, 19 March. Available at https://www.standard.co.uk/news/uk/naga-munchetty-union-flag-tweet-b925026.html.

[3] Sparrow, Andrew (2009), 'Cameron faces calls to disown Hannan NHS 'mistake' criticism' *Guardian*, 5 April. Available at https://www.theguardian.com/politics/2009/apr/05/cameron-hannan-nhs-prescott.

partisanship. Almost 15 years ago, senior executives began to frame its maxim of 'due impartiality' to one of 'radical impartiality' to allow more fringe views airtime on the free speech principle that the public sector broadcaster should more widely reflect the range of opinions of the licence payers in the country as a whole. The rot soon set in...

It's not just that more extremist views were heard, or for the sake of balance that Nigel Farage had a near-permanent seat on BBC *Question Time*. In a sense, the 'balance' of political commentary didn't matter. More devastating was the influence on reflecting opinion rather than fact, and turning the public broadcaster into some huge *Vox Pop* at the expense of its core Reithian function - to entertain, educate and inform.

As BBC stalwarts, like former producer and reporter Patrick Howse, have pointed out: "The BBC is confusing factuality with balance. The truth is not the midpoint between a fact and a lie."[1] As BBC News presenter Clive Myrie, in his lecture in honour of the late Harold Evans, put it: "What is journalism for? The short answer: truth."[2]

Some truths are inalienable. Our broadcasting technology wouldn't even exist if the world was flat. Our daily news would cease to be the first draft of history if key historical events like the Holocaust were denied. Objectivity is not neutrality, and though we may never achieve the absolute zero of truth, journalists can still be guided by it, just as travellers have used the Pole Star to navigate, without actually visiting Polaris.

Instead of providing a beacon to the UK, the BBC decided to become a mirror of the nation and therefore opened itself up to all the tricks of lobbying groups, grotesque threats from politicians, and a wilderness of opinions about opinions, reflections on reflections, until the whole point of its existence is in doubt.

---

[1] Howse, Patrick (2020), 'The Power of Populist Lies and the BBC's Failure to Expose Them', *Byline Times*, 10 November. Available at
https://bylinetimes.com/2020/11/10/us-election-2020-the-power-of-populist-lies-and-the-bbcs-failure-to-expose-them/.

[2] Myrie, Clive (2021), 'What is journalism for? The short answer: truth', *Guardian*, 11 March. Available at
https://www.theguardian.com/commentisfree/2021/mar/11/journalism-truth-strong-regulation-us-media-uk.

(Not) 'Going Native'?

But who will guide it out of this maze? Back in the 80s, the belief was that even a Conservative grandee like Marmaduke Hussey would 'go native' once installed as Chairman and there's no reason to assume that Tim Davie, even though he is a former Conservative Party candidate, couldn't also defend the corporation's principles. But he reports to Richard Sharp, a former Goldman Sachs banker who donated £400,000[1] to the Conservative Party.

Ultimately, the defence of BBC standards will rest with the new chair of *Ofcom*. That Paul Dacre, former editor of the *Daily Mail*, is being suggested for the post may be an epic case of trolling liberal opinion by Government sources. As Julian Petley explains in this book,[2] Dacre has long derided both the BBC and the concept of independent regulation of journalism and is hardly an avatar of impartiality or objectivity. But the fact that he is even mooted is a sign that the culture wars around commentary are dominant, rather than what actually made the BBC such a global brand and a power that repressive governments abroad had to reckon with: as a source of accurate information.

About the Contributor

Peter Jukes is the founder and executive editor of *Byline Times*. He is a playwright and literary critic and is the author of *Beyond Contempt: The Inside story of the Phone Hacking Trial* (Canbury Press, 2014).

---

[1] Bright, Sam (2021). 'New BBC Chairman has Donated Over £400,000 to the Conservative Party', *Byline Times,* 6 January. Available at https://bylinetimes.com/2021/01/06/new-bbc-chairman-richard-sharp-donated-more-than-400000-to-conservative-party/.

[2] Petley, Julian (2021), 'Paul Dacre, Ofcom and the Coming of the Post-Nolan Era'.

Section Three
Priorities For The New Chair

John Mair

The shadow of Paul Dacre hangs over the future of *Ofcom* like a ghost. He may have thrown his hat in to be chair. He may not have done. We won't know until the (Not) Fat Secretary of State sings! Whoever is offered and takes the job, there will be a sharp right turn in direction. That's the modus operandi of the Johnson government – scare, be outrageous then pull back and be seen to be 'reasonable'.

Ofcom is at a cross roads as it prepares to enter its third decade. Huge responsibilities are to be thrust on it to take on the FAANGS(The Tech Giants) on online harm and market power. The challenges are huge.

Paul Connew, the distinguished Fleet Street editor turned media commentator comes over all Shakespearean in his examination of '***The Ides of March'*** – the unceremonious exit of Piers Morgan from *Good Morning Britain* over his on-air mauling of the Duchess of Sussex about her Oprah interview. He stormed off the set and flounced out of the company – a regular Piers habit. Complaints flooded in to *Ofcom*, Chief among them a missal from one M. Markel of San Bernadino California USA. It is a tricky one!

Philip Collins used to be at the centre of power in Downing Street. He was Tony Blair's chief speech-writer. He is now a journalistic observer of the Boris Johnson Show. He looks askance at one of the latest wheezes – the idea of the 'populist' former editor of the Daily Mail as *Ofcom* chair. In '**Why NOT to make Paul Dacre the story rather than a regulator**' he points out that Dacre is uniquely unqualified for the job.

Professor Julian Petley is another Dacre Dissenter. His beef is over the Johnson government riding roughshod over the Nolan rules on public appointments to ensure they are fair and transparent. The *Ofcom* Chair being the latest in a disturbing trend in the 'Post Nolan era'.

Finally, Christopher Williams, business editor of the whole *Telegraph* stable and a seasoned *Ofcom* watcher, finds *Ofcom* behind the curve in both broadcasting and telephony.

This is a good book end to a volume which started with a job application from a Court of Appeal judge and ends who knows where. Maybe the broadcasting Wild West is coming to the UK? Watch this space.

Chapter Thirteen

Ofcom, beware the Ides of March

Paul Connew muses how, given the fall-out from <u>that</u> Oprah interview coincided with the Ides of March, Shakespeare could have interpreted the drama.

By the time the Ides of March arrived on March 15 2021 I was haunted by a thought: If only Shakespeare were here to chronicle the events and fallout of that 'bombshell' Oprah Winfrey interview with the Duke and Duchess of Sussex (aka 'Haz and Meg').

It had everything The Immortal Bard could have wished for by way of plotlines. Royal intrigue, betrayal, brutal assassination (of the character variety), chaos, elements of tragedy and comedy. Efforts to portray the whole thing as a much ado about nothing soap opera had come to nought as a veritable rage engulfed the court of public and media opinion.

In Ancient Rome, the Ides of March marked the time to settle debts. In the 2021 media world, it marked the time for settling scores.

What, I mused, would Our Will have made of a royal prince and his wife branding one of the two heirs to the throne a heartless racist?

Queen Oprah: More courtier than interrogator

How would he have cast 'Queen Oprah', the famed interviewer from across the ocean who oft appeared to have assumed the role of pliant courtier providing a PR platform and abandoning all pretence of forensic interrogator and assuming that of both juror and judge?

Not least with her CBS network partner showing incendiary/racist headlines from foreign papers, including US supermarket scandal sheets, to give the impression they were from Harry and Meghan's bête noir British tabloids. (British newspapers can certainly be guilty of racism and bigotry, with evidence to prove it, but not on the institutional, uniform scale claimed by the Sussexes. It was healthy that a membership revolt sparked the resignation of the Society of Editors' Executive Director Ian Murray for foolishly issuing an unsustainable kneejerk blanket acquittal statement in response to the Oprah interview).

So how would the Immortal Bard have interpreted the 'End of the Piers Show' (well, on ITV breakfast, anyway)? Would he have cast Mr Morgan as popular hero, stoutly defending Queen and country against the slings and arrows of outrageous (mis)fortune or as an overly proud and petulant opportunist?

Or how indeed would he script the tricky role (and future) of *Ofcom* amid all this turmoil? Apart, presumably, from pondering the only (head-shedding) regulator he had to deal with back in the day was the risk of displeasing the reigning monarch personally.

All hail Dacre?

How would he have played a plot twist where Paul Dacre, avowed critic of the BBC and vehement opponent of state regulation of newspapers, was the Prime Minister's choice to head the broadcast regulator *Ofcom*? (At the time of writing my sources tell me that, although Boris Johnson is still taken with the idea of appointing Dacre, senior Tory soothsayers are advising him against it and that the odds are 'now no better, or worse, than 50/50 either way').

On a measure for measure basis, a reincarnated Shakespeare might have to juggle a script around *Ofcom* receiving a record 57,000-plus complaints (more than the regulator's entire complaints log for the year) about the aforementioned Piers Morgan within days, and with petitions totalling around 250,000 demanding his reinstatement on the *Good Morning Britain* breakfast stage?

Not to mention the contradiction between the Morgan departure wiping £200m off ITV*'s* share value and shedding up to 250,000 of GMB's audience ratings with the 12 million who tuned in to the Oprah interview, with an advertiser boost that justified the reported £1m UK screening rights deal and (arguably) the social media/publicity firestorm it ignited.

The End of the Piers Show...not

On the thorny subject of Piers Morgan, let me make my position clear. In a previous book in this series I saluted him as going from 'liberal zero to hero' for his standout role in holding government ministers to account over their handling of the Covid crisis and then mercilessly mocking them in absentia when they boycotted GMB. I stand solidly by that.

For the record I also thought Morgan was justified in flagging up the obvious factual flaws in the Sussexes' Oprah interview and in Winfrey's failure to probe and challenge their version of events. Reasonable, too, to question why a couple championing the cause of privacy were so apparently addicted to (global) publicity.

This was legitimate broadcast journalism and contrasted favourably with the journalistic sloppiness of some BBC News bulletins that referred to Harry and Meghan's 'revelations' and 'disclosures' NOT, alas, 'claims' or 'allegations' or 'accusations'.

But what compromised Morgan's position was the painful running 'joke' on the show for months about him being personally 'ghosted' by Ms Markle after she met Prince Harry. Inevitably, many female critics in both the main stream media and on social media accused Morgan of being 'creepily obsessive' about her. A charge apparently laid by some *Ofcom* complainants.

Morgan's Breakfast Megxit

Funnily enough, it was a point I was discussing live on a BBC radio interview when the news broke that Morgan had stormed off set in that headline-hitting row with weather presenter colleague Alex Beresford. At first, I thought it was a stunt but the replay footage promptly changed my mind.

It was a mistake by Morgan, particularly in the sense that he who revels in dishing it out has to be able to take it. But where I seriously disagreed with Piers -- and said so on air -- is that neither he nor I know the truth or otherwise of Meghan's account of mental woes and suicidal thoughts and to publicly call her a liar wasn't just unacceptable but dangerous in its wider mental health implications. (The latter point Meghan smartly seized on both in her initial informal complaint to ITV CEO Dame Carolyn McCall and her subsequent formal complaint to *Ofcom*).

It then became inevitable that Morgan would walk (or be shoved) after McCall announced she believed everything Meghan had said and Morgan predictably refused to apologise and doubled down on Twitter and doorstep TV interviews, strategically casting himself as the 'free speech' martyr taking on a dishonest royal bride. Certainly Twitter was full of voices championing the Marmite Man's opinionated, 'shock jock', *Ofcom* stress-testing style of presenting over the BBC's safer, blander breakfast fayre.

The steadily reducing ratings gap between BBC Breakfast and *Good Morning Britain* prior to Morgan's departure bore witness to that, as Piers constantly reminded us.

So why does my Shakespearean flight of fantasy matter in the context of a book about *Ofcom*? Well, apart from anything else in the immediate fallout from the Oprah furore, Morgan's Megxit from ITV breakfast looks set to be followed by him signing up for a lucrative starring role on one of the two new British TV news channels.

The idea of Piers as a self-anointed Messiah of 'free speech' might well see his critics gearing up to put *Ofcom* to the test on a regular basis.

Testing times ahead for *Ofcom*

With conservative platforms and professed 'anti-woke, anti-cancel culture, anti-snowflake' agendas, and controversial backing from overseas investors with deep pockets and conservative pedigrees, the role, and indeed the long-term future of *Ofcom*, is set to be put to the test like never before.

Indeed the redoubtable Andrew Neil, powerful front man for GB News, openly courted hiring Morgan in an interview with Sky News. While less publicly Piers' former boss, Rupert Murdoch, was working on recruiting him for his rival *UK TV* platform. Morgan's brand appeal doubtless boosted by his book, *Wake Up: Why the 'liberal' war on free speech is even more dangerous than COVID-19* reaching Number One on the Amazon best-seller list.

On March 28 Morgan was boosted by a front-page blurb and a remarkable 4 pages inside the Mail on Sunday to tell the 'inside story' of his GMB departure and heavily promote/market his cause celebre (anti-woke credentials).

The Murdoch offer, rumour has it, would be combined with a role with Fox News in the US - although quite how that would sit with the strongly pro-Trump audience, doubtless aware that the presenter dropped his previously fawning stance on The Donald to become a ferocious critic over his catastrophic pandemic failures, remains to be seen. Piers' estimable CNN back story campaigning against US gun laws wouldn't exactly match the Fox News audience profile either!

For his part, Andrew Neil has publicly insisted GB News will be *'Ofcom compliant'*. Quite how that comes to be defined-and tested is the big question. Murdoch's UKTV will pose the same testing question. Both channels will promote themselves as the alternative voice to the 'liberal metropolitan elite' they contend dominate the UK media and as the combative champions of the 'ordinary' man and woman.

Impartiality on the line

In his eloquent March 11 lecture in honour of Sir Harold Evans, the award-winning BBC journalist Clive Myrie took as his theme: *'Over here, over there: Lessons from the USA. Why TV journalism needs to be fair and impartial.'*

Myrie argued the importance of *Ofcom*, while acknowledging that such eminent broadcast figures as former BBC, ITV and Channel 4 boss Michael Grade are more sceptical. He also made considerable play of how a certain James Murdoch once argued a MacTaggart Lecture case for dispensing with broadcast regulation and leaving it down to market forces.

This is the same James Murdoch, Myrie noted, who has now undergone a Damascene conversion and fallen out with the Fox News channel he once co-headed for his father, and whose position he implicitly condemned on Trump, right wing politics generally and, most explicitly, Fox's record on climate change issues, among others.

But those sharing Myrie's opinion might have felt a frisson of concern over the words of Adam Baxter, *Ofcom*'s director of standards and audience protection, in the wake of the Meghan/Harry/Oprah/Morgan melodrama.

Suffice to say, Shakespeare could make rich play of Baxter's title and tortured role to come against the backdrop of GB News and UKTV's market entry and a social media firestorm in which support for Piers Morgan's defiant 'right to rant' was running at least as strongly as those damning him.

'There is no absolute right not to be offended by what you see on TV and hear on radio', declared Baxter, triggering headlines like 'GB News can be right wing and offend viewers within impartiality rules'.

Foxification...to be or not to be?

In what some might see as a move toward a more elastic interpretation of 'due impartiality' or even a drift toward the 'Foxification' of British news broadcasting, Baxter stated 'Due impartiality does not mean some mathematical construct where representative of Group A has to be given equal airtime to representative of Group B'.

Of the new Neil/Murdoch channels he said: 'People have said about the new channels, 'Oh my God, isn't this awful'. We're alive to that debate. Both are seeking to come from a right of centre perspective and there's nothing in the code that prohibits a broadcaster coming from a particular perspective.

'Both new services have been awarded a licence by *Ofcom* and have been keen to stress their commitment to due impartiality. We think broadcasters should have the freedom and lassitude to decide how they achieve that'.

I'm a liberal, moderately left of centre commentator who tends to sympathise with Baxter, given our rapidly evolving media landscape, the era of *Netflix, Amazon, Disney +,Apple TV* et al, and with the omnipresent social media influence hard to discount in the *Ofcom* equation.

Personally, I'm less taxed by the arrival of *GB News* and UKTV than the question: Where are the progressive investors willing and able to launch left-leaning rival stations?

I suspect a fellow man of Warwickshire by the name of Will would agree... if only he were around to air an opinion.

Note on the Author

Paul Connew is a media commentator/advisor, broadcaster, ex-editor of Sunday *Mirror* and deputy editor of the *Daily Mirror*, a columnist with *The New European* and *The Drum*. He comments on media issues for the BBC, Sky News, CNN, Talk Radio, Times Radio, LBC, Al-Jazeera, ABC and CBC. A longstanding Society of Editors member, and awards judge, Connew was among those who publicly disowned the SoE's original statement denying racism existed at all in the UK press.

Chapter Fourteen

Why NOT to make Paul Dacre the story rather than a regulator

Philip Collins has been at the centre of power in Downing Street with Tony Blair. He looks askance at the idea of Paul Dacre as *Ofcom* chair.

In a speech delivered before he became Prime Minister, David Cameron said that *Ofcom* in its current incarnation would not survive a Conservative government. Mr Cameron shied away from the mooted reform once he came to office but, a decade and a half later, the threat seems to be current again. Though Boris Johnson has not been as explicit as his predecessor as Prime Minister, the regular whispers that he intends to appoint Paul Dacre, former editor of *The Daily Mail and* editor-in-chief of Associated Newspapers, to the chairmanship of *Ofcom*, the communications regulator, suggest that the threat has returned.

Boris is not Dave!

The motivation now is importantly different. Mr Cameron was making the case that communications were part of the public realm and that policy making should therefore be under political control. He therefore proposed returning policy to the Department of Culture, Media and Sport and leaving *Ofcom* as a rather dry enforcement and invigilation body. Mr Johnson appears to be inspired by motives that are less easy to dignify with philosophical support. He seems to think that broadcasting needs shaking up, that it has become the preserve of the politically correct and that a little populist dissent might be all to the good.

There are two reasons why both Mr Cameron and Mr Johnson are wrong about *Ofcom* and why an expert chair would be preferable to a self-styled dissident. Broadcasting is, first, a technical question and the regulators need to be across an enormous array of detail. Second and more importantly, the precious inheritance of British broadcasting is that it seeks to protect an idea of neutrality. To appoint an evident partisan at the top of the regulatory regime is a signal that the government does not understand what makes British broadcasting as good as anywhere in the world.

Neutrality rules at *Ofcom*

The appointments of the senior personnel at *Ofcom*, since the body was formed in 2003, have generally had specific regard for the principle of neutrality. The authority in *Ofcom* really lies with the chief executive and all the incumbents so far – Stephen Carter, Ed Richards, Sharon White and Melanie Dawes – have all negotiated political controversy with ease. They have all been assisted in that by chairs of a scrupulously neutral kind.

The departing chair Terry Burns, for example, is an experienced mandarin figure. Though his predecessors Patricia Hodgson and David Currie had loose associations with the Conservative and Labour parties respectively, neither were at all known for their politics and both had a wealth of relevant experience in the trade. They contrast very markedly with Paul Dacre who, lacking relevant experience in those fields of the media over which *Ofcom* adjudicates, really brings to the table only a capacity for controversy and not much else.

Sir Alan Moses, until recently the chair of the Independent Press Standards Organization, put the point nicely when he said that, if he were appointed, Dacre might find the joke is on him. Moses's point is that the chair of *Ofcom* is a managerial rather than an executive role and that the work that needs doing is technical and complex. The implication is that someone like Paul Dacre would be bored to tears by most of what *Ofcom* actually does (See Alan Moses Chapter one in this book).

What can Dacre bring to the table?

Take a look at the *Ofcom* agenda and ask yourself whether a former newspaper editor has anything to add to the debate. The crucial question of investment in faster and universal broadband, for example, requires an immersion in the complex and technical economic literature. Broadband speed will prove to be a much bigger issue than whether the content of the *10 O'clock News* is biased. The consumer law that pertains to ensuring broadband, TV and phone customers can switch easily is difficult and important. Then there are all the applications for Code powers, licence exemption for wireless telegraphy devices and the modifications to the USP access conditions for regulating the Royal Mail's postal network.

These are all subjects of recent publications by *Ofcom*. This is the agenda that the new chairman inherits. It is a specialist job and it needs someone who knows what they are doing.

The obvious risk is that a celebrity chair without relevant expertise might be inclined to interfere in that fraction of *Ofcom's* business which interests him. Mr. Dacre has made no secret of his loathing for the large tech companies and, though there is plenty to be said about the way they operate, it is not obvious that the chair of the regulatory body is the person to say it. The government has indicated that *Ofcom* will be appointed the regulator for online harms, to protect users from harmful and illegal conduct. This is a statutory role demanding impartiality. This is no job for a partisan.

Putting the BBC in its place? Upsetting the ecology of good broadcasting

The other part of the job that might intrigue Mr Dacre is, of course, broadcasting. *Ofcom* licences all commercial television and radio services in the UK. It publishes the Broadcasting Code, a set of rules which all broadcasters must follow. *Ofcom* also now has a new role in monitoring and reporting on the BBC and this is the only part of the job which would animate Dacre. It is the part of the job that seems to animate a certain type of Conservative who is always convinced that the BBC is a nest of socialists cleverly pumping out propaganda that brainwashes the nation into mindless Left-wingery.

In truth, public service broadcasting is one of the few industries that Britain does to a world-class standard. This is not just about the BBC, of course. Public service broadcasting extends to ITV, Channel 4, and Channel Five (and Sky News) and it is something of which we should be proud. It is often said that British news coverage compares favourably with that of, say, the United States of America, and it is said often because it is true. Imagine the Brexit saga played out on partial news channels. It would have been even more awful than it was in any case. Though the BBC's coverage excited a great deal of criticism – tellingly from both sides – it was, in truth, dull, unimaginative but not especially biased.

The 'Foxification' of British TV news?

The principle of neutrality, which is what makes BBC/ITN/Sky news coverage work, is now under threat. Two new channels, *GB News* and a rival created by Rupert Murdoch, are about to join the broadcasting spectrum. The people behind them expressly say, with tedious regularity and no supporting evidence, that British broadcasting needs to be freed from its suffocating liberal biases. What they mean by this is that they want their licence to be opinionated, which is just what broadcasting regulation does not allow. It is true, of course, that the selection of information reveals implicit bias. The coverage of some news stories rather than others illustrates a manner of thinking. That said, this is still a long way from television news with opinions.

As a country we have always recognized that our public conversation is better conducted in a neutral venue. What problem does anyone think is being addressed with the creation of partisan news? It would be to undermine the very thing that has made British news broadcasting respected around the world. It would be a strange act of self-sabotage. The best appointment to the chair at *Ofcom* would be one that did not itself make the news because that would mean that the new man or woman at the top had the technical expertise to do the job well and had no interest in becoming a story.

About the Contributor

Philip Collins is the former chief speechwriter for Prime Minister Tony Blair. He was then a columnist on *The Times*. They let him go in 2020 allegedly for being 'too left wing'. He wore that badge with pride. 'I've always wanted to be thought too left wing but never thought I would achieve it' he said in his farewell email. He is now a writer and contributing editor for the *New Statesman* and has his own company *Draftwriters.*

Chapter Fifteen

Paul Dacre, *Ofcom*, and the Coming of the Post-Nolan Era

The Johnson government is nothing if not radical – even after Dominic Cummings' departure. And it loves to fly populist kites to see if they take off. One of the latest is the idea of uber Right winger Paul Dacre to chair Ofcom. *Professor Julian Petley.*

Imagine a bank appointing a confirmed Marxist as its CEO, or an oil company doing likewise with a passionate campaigner against fossil fuels. Sounds crazy? Indeed it does, but it's no crazier than the present government wanting to appoint Paul Dacre as the head of *Ofcom,* an organisation which, like the BBC, he has made no secret of absolutely loathing.

Dacre's jeremiads against the BBC have been permanent fixtures at the Daily Mail ever since he became its editor in 1992, and these continued unabated until he stepped down in 2018. Thereafter he not only retained the role of editor-in-chief of Associated Newspapers, which publishes the Daily Mail and the Mail on Sunday, but also became its chairman. And yet, as chair of *Ofcom*, Dacre may have considerable power over the hated BBC because, since 2017, it has been the Corporation's first external regulator, and, as such, is responsible for setting the operating framework and licence for its' UK services.

The idea of putting a BBC hater in charge of its regulator is bizarre enough. But less well-known is the fact that Dacre is an *Ofcom*-hater as well.

'The worst kind of bloated quango': Dacre on *Ofcom*

Back in 2011, the *Mail* worked itself up to fever pitch over *Ofcom*'s refusal to censure an episode of ITV's *The X Factor*, broadcast the previous December, which featured raunchy numbers involving Rihanna and Christine Aguilera. *Ofcom* received 2,868 complaints, but research by the regulator revealed that 2,000 of these came from readers of the *Mail*, whose article about the show 'contained significantly more graphic material than had actually been broadcast' (*Ofcom* 2011). After *Ofcom* not only refused to censure the programme but criticised the distorting effect of the *Mail*'s coverage on its complaints log (albeit without mentioning the paper by name), Dacre and his staff went into full-on outrage overdrive.

Thus the *Mail* comment column, 22 April 2011, accused *Ofcom* of 'shameful sophistry' and argued that 'the truth is this body, with its 870 staff and Labour crony chief executive Ed Richards (pay packet £380,000) is the worst kind of bloated quango' and reminded readers that 'in opposition Mr Cameron promised that, under the Tories, "*Ofcom* would be dramatically slimmed down". That day cannot come soon enough'. A further article the following day noted that 'David Cameron has made *Ofcom* a firm target for the proposed "Bonfire of the Quangos", vowing in 2009 that "with a Conservative government, *Ofcom* as we know it will cease to exist"' (Seamark and Thomas 2011). A comment column on 4 June 2011 headed 'Pathetic *Ofcom* and Our Vulnerable Young' lambasted it as a 'politically correct, toothless regulator'.

Dacre's split personality on media regulation.

However, although Dacre clearly believes that the statutory regulation of broadcasting is far too 'permissive', he himself is a virulent opponent of any form of statutory press regulation, branding the Leveson-compliant press regulator Impress a 'joke body' and wholly inaccurately describing it as 'the Government's press regulator funded by Max Mosley' (Ponsford 2016). Of course, it might be argued that since the press and broadcasting are entirely different forms of media they should be regulated in different ways, but this would be to ignore the fact that much of the output of both the press and broadcasting is journalism. And this means that Dacre's journalistic record is highly relevant to the question of whether he is fit to chair *Ofcom*.

The evidence (Cathcart 2021) would strongly suggest not, and this in spite of the fact that from 2008 to 2016 Dacre was chair of the Editors' Code Committee, which draws up the standards code formerly policed by the Press Complaints Commission (PCC) and since 2014 by the Independent Press Standards Organisation (IPSO). Indeed, in the year Dacre took up this role, Nick Davies in *Flat Earth* News (2008) revealed that his analysis of ten years of the PCC's records demonstrated that during that time the *Mail* had been 'provoking justifiable complaint about unethical behaviour at just over three times the rate of the other national titles'. Nor have its journalistic standards improved in the years since. To take but one example (Cathcart 2014), in 2013 the PCC received 1,214 complaints about the *Mail*, accounting for 36.4% of the total number of complaints about all the national dailies. (The Sun, which was second on the list, had 638 complaints – 19.1% of the total).

The Nolan Committee on Standards in Public Life

But if Paul Dacre is so manifestly unsuited to chair a media regulatory body, how is it that he is being seriously considered for the job? One answer is that this is part of the Tories' culture war – a calculated slap in the face to liberal opinion. However, the real significance of Dacre's proposed appointment is that it is yet another sign that we have entered the post-Nolan era.

As a result of the cash-for-questions affair and other sleazy episodes in the 1990s, John Major set up the Committee on Standards in Public Life (1995) under the chairmanship of Lord Nolan. Among the many causes for unease at the time was that appointments were being made to public bodies for political reasons without due process, and that appointees were coming from a narrow circle of candidates. Nolan decided that a Commissioner for Public Appointments should be appointed, who would establish a Code of Practice for public appointments and regulate the system according to the Code. But while the committee concluded that ministers should remain accountable for public appointments, it also recommended a long line of checks and balances on this exercise of ministerial power. This included the requirements that 'all public appointments should be governed by the overriding principle of appointment on merit'; that 'each panel or committee should have at least one independent member and independent members should normally account for at least a third of membership'; and that 'the Public Appointments Commissioner should monitor, regulate and approve departmental appointments procedures'.

Laying the Foundations of the Post-Nolan Era

Ever since the Tories came to power in 2010, the role of the Commissioner has gradually been reduced and political patronage in the making of public appointments has once again increased. Partly as a result of bodies such as *Conservative Home* and the *Tax Payers' Alliance* endlessly complaining that public bodies were stuffed with

'Tony's cronies', after the Tories clearly won the 2015 election, enabling them to dump their erstwhile Lib Dem coalition partners, they established a review of the Commissioner's office. This was led by Sir Gerry Grimstone, a former director of Barclays plc and Standard Life (and now a Conservative peer). He concluded that the appointments process was too bureaucratic and recommended that many of the Commissioner's functions should be reduced. The government agreed, and so the machinery was set in place for what is now widely regarded as the Johnson government's routine use of the public appointments system for the purposes of political or personal patronage: in other words, populating the 'chumocracy'.

The present situation was the subject of a letter by the outgoing Commissioner, Peter Riddell, to Lord Evans, Chair of the Committee on Standards in Public Life, on 7 October 2020 (Riddell 2020a). Here he stressed the fact that in the appointments process, 'ministers can at all stages suggest candidates and have the final say but their choice is constrained by a system of fair and open competition in which all candidates are treated equally'. This is a balancing act that has always 'depended on restraint and good sense. For instance, ministers have respected the results of competitions and have not sought to use the provisions to appoint a candidate judged un-appointable by the interview panel'. Candidates' political activity is no bar to their being appointed, but 'the key is that they are not appointed just as a result of patronage but emerge from a rigorous comparison with other candidates on the basis of a fair and open competition'.

This, at least, is how the system has generally worked up until recently, even after the Commissioner's role was greatly reduced post-Grimstone. But according to Riddell, there are signs that this balance is under threat, because 'some at the centre of government want not only to have the final say but to tilt the competition system in their favour to appoint their allies'.

In this respect, he noted that on several recent occasions he has had to resist attempts by ministers to appoint people with clear party affiliations as Senior Independent Panel Members when that is expressly barred under the Code. There have also been attempts to stretch the Code by, for example, packing the composition of interview panels with allies, notably in the current case of the panel for the competition of the Office for Students, which has a panel of five where there is no one with senior recent experience of higher education or a student involved.

It's worth adding here that the panel included former Tory councillor Baroness Wyld, former Tory candidate Patricia Hodgson, and Nick Timothy, former chief of staff to Tory PM Theresa May. In the event the job went to the Tory peer Lord Wharton, the former manager of Boris Johnson's leadership campaign, and someone with absolutely no relevant educational experience. Unlike, that is, the unsuccessful candidate Sir Ivor Crewe, the former vice-chancellor of the University of Essex, one-time head of Universities UK and then master of University College, Oxford.

Softening Up? Trailing Names in Friendly Papers

In his evidence to the Public Administration and Constitutional Affairs Committee on 8 October, Riddell (2020b) also expressed concern at the names of the government's preferred candidates for certain public appointments being trailed in friendly newspapers prior to the formal appointments process. Here he mentioned Dacre specifically, along with Charles Moore, who was at one time being touted as the new BBC Chairman.

Whilst not criticising the individuals themselves, he nonetheless stated that floating 'apparently authoritatively inspired' press stories about them was 'extremely unhelpful' and 'prejudices the whole system'. This is because it gives the impression that there is an officially preferred candidate for the post, which discourages others from even applying.

In February 2021 it became clear that Paul Potts, appointed two years ago as an independent director of Times Newspapers Holdings, would be the senior independent panel member on the *Ofcom* appointments panel. This is the clearest possible indication of the dangers to the public appointments system made possible by Grimstone and actualised by the Johnson government, since it is extremely difficult to understand in what possible sense Potts can be considered 'independent'. Not only is the Murdoch press quite as hostile to the BBC as are the *Mail* titles, but Potts is a former business associate at the SWNS Media Group of the DCMS minister for media and data, John Whittingdale, whose anti-BBC credentials are not exactly a secret (Geoghegan and Cusick 2020).

Lack of Political and Constitutional Self-restraint

The government's attempts to manoeuvre Dacre into the *Ofcom* chairmanship epitomise precisely those processes of untrammelled and unaccountable political patronage in the process of public appointments that Lord Nolan's committee wanted to see expunged from public life. But, as we have seen, the Dacre case is by no means an isolated example. It is an acute symptom of what David Allen Green (2021) has called 'the lack of political and constitutional self-restraint' which is laid bare when ministers no longer feel obliged to act according to the customary norms of Peter Hennessy's famous 'good chaps theory of government'. As Green argues, what ministers are now doing is 'showing openly what the constitution of the United Kingdom has long been capable of permitting', and, as things stand, there appears to be very little that can be done about it, other than drawing public attention to these profoundly disturbing developments.

About the Contributor

Julian Petley is emeritus and honorary professor of journalism at Brunel University London. His most recent book is the second edition of *Culture Wars: The Media and the British Left* (Routledge 2019), co-written with James Curran and Ivor Gaber. He is a member of the editorial board of the *British Journalism Review* and the principal editor of the *Journal of British Cinema and Television*. A former journalist, he now contributes to online publications such as *Inforrm*, *Byline Times* and *open Democracy*.

Chapter Sixteen

Ofcom: Firmly a bystander to history in television and in telephony

Simply unfit for the modern world of television streamers and technology leaps in broadband. That's the view of *Telegraph* Business Editor Christopher Williams who has reported the regulator for close to a decade.

There was a swagger about *Ofcom* that was not unjustified. In early 2014, when I was invited to meet its chief executive Ed Richards, the regulator seemed to be master of its markets and politically unassailable.

Richards, who as a policy adviser to Tony Blair had played a crucial role in *Ofcom's* creation, had gone on to successfully steer the organisation through some treacherous waters. David Cameron had gone into the 2010 election with the promise to curtail its powers such that "*Ofcom* as we know it will cease to exist".

Southwark Bridge Road supreme

Instead, the inhabitants of 2a Southwark Bridge Road were more powerful than ever. *Ofcom's* work investigating and delaying News Corp's attempted takeover of Sky had proved pivotal, allowing the ugly extent of the phone hacking scandal to be revealed.

As public revulsion engulfed the Murdoch newspapers in July 2011, Richards decided to remind News Corp of his duty to assess whether it would be a 'fit and proper' holder of a broadcasting licence.

It was nearly the final blow to the bid and by standing up to the world's most powerful media baron, he had made *Ofcom* almost untouchable. Far from losing powers, in the years since it has gained oversight of the BBC and is soon to take on the vastness of the web as regulator of harmful online content.

Yet in that time, during which I have continually covered *Ofcom* for The Telegraph, there has been a noticeable decline in its relevance, especially to the television industry. I suspect this is partly an ironic result of its actions in the phone hacking scandal.

Politicians wary of changing *Ofcom*

Fearful of the stink that still wafts from that midden, politicians have failed to change *Ofcom* even as the industries it is meant to regulate have been utterly transformed. To a great extent *Netflix*, *Amazon*, *YouTube* and *Disney+* operate beyond the reach of Britain's television watchdog. Perhaps that is acceptable, but it has never been seriously discussed.

Cameron could never go anywhere near media legislation, thanks to his many personal embarrassments at the Leveson Inquiry. In any case, he led a coalition and a Conservative government that were bewitched by the American technology companies benefiting from an outdated regime of oversight.

The convulsions of Brexit and minority government meant Theresa May had neither the time nor the appetite to address issues which are highly controversial among elites but do not stir ordinary voters.

We now have a government which seems very interested in media regulation, but doesn't seem determined to reform its legislation or structures. Instead, Boris Johnson has brought a focus on the appointment of senior personnel deemed politically acceptable.

When *Ofcom's* directors wanted to appoint Melanie Dawes as chief executive, they were effectively ordered back to the drawing board by Number 10, where advisers including Dominic Cummings believed a candidate with a more commercial background was required. The career civil servant was ultimately given the job after failed attempts to drum up interest from senior industry figures who would have been required to take a large pay cut. In exchange, Downing Street wanted a more radical chairman than the incumbent Terry Burns, another Whitehall veteran.

The TV world has changed around *Ofcom*

Yet without new laws, whoever is running *Ofcom* will gain most influence over a corner of the television universe that is shrinking and alarmed. The broadcasting business is losing financial and cultural clout - in both relative and absolute terms - at a rate that frightens those in its upper ranks. They look to *Ofcom* for help, which impotently calls for collaboration between broadcasters and looks to the government for new powers to level the pitch as they seek to compete with tech giants. Nothing of any significance changes.

This has been the pattern of the last few years and a big source of frustration for *Ofcom*. There are few signs of imminent change. The regulator's review of public service broadcasting last year amounted to a desperate appeal for powers.

The economic and legislative pile-up caused by coronavirus means senior broadcasting executives now expect ministers to act fast to address what *Ofcom* said was an urgent and existential threat to British broadcasting. By the time new laws are in place (not this year or next) there will be less left to save. As an economic regulator of broadcasting with almost no power over streaming, *Ofcom* is a bystander to the biggest competitive challenge the industry has ever faced.

Ofcom's first self-inflicted wound: Broadband

The politicians are not solely to blame for *Ofcom*'s struggle to respond to the changes in its markets, however. The regulator has also taken decisions that betray self-satisfaction rather than desire to understand the businesses it regulates and embrace change, particularly in telecoms.

In the mid-2000s *Ofcom* forced BT's network arm Openreach to allow rival broadband providers to install their own computer equipment in local telephone exchanges. It was a massive regulatory success, creating strong retail competition which drove down prices and expanded the market. However, as the market matured BT began making bigger returns while providing dismal service.

It took a determined campaign by rivals, politicians and media to force *Ofcom* to act. Its broadband policy had been an international calling card, and even as technology and competitive dynamics changed radically, it tinkered around the edges.

Under a new chief executive, Sharon White, *Ofcom* eventually imposed a legal separation of Openreach from the rest of BT in 2017, which has improved matters. But Britain still lags other economies in the rollout of "full fibre" broadband. The upgrade would replace the aged copper wire connecting each home to the network with a much faster and more reliable fibre-optic connection.

Ofcom was slow to appreciate the need for the upgrade even as other European economies forged ahead. Once it did, the regulator decided to encourage a race to build competing networks. Yet the policy, which previously proved effective in mobile telecoms, is struggling to deliver full fibre against the wishes of established big players including Sky, due to some characteristics of a 'natural monopoly' like the water system or power network.

Years into the rollout, with coverage just creeping into double digits, *Ofcom* shows no sign that it is willing to recant.

The second self-inflicted wound: Mobile mergers

This attitude was most starkly on show when the mobile operators O2 and Three attempted to merge in 2016. *Ofcom*, with its faith in competing infrastructure, was convinced, against the advice of some of the experts on its board, that Britain required four separate mobile operators.

In collaboration with the European Commission, which then had legal oversight of the deal, *Ofcom* acted to block a merger which it claimed would have led to an increase in prices for consumers. Three and O2 argued the combination would have cut costs which would have allowed more investment in mobile coverage, but were overruled, even though the combination would have given a leg up to Sky as a new competitive force in the market.

Four years later, the European Commission suffered an unusual defeat in the European Court of Justice, which ruled that its economic analysis - and *Ofcom's* - had been faulty. A deal which could have accelerated Britain's digital economy was needlessly blocked. It is hard to escape the conclusion that *Ofcom* was just too pleased with the market it had created.

Looking backwards to the future?

There is a common thread in *Ofcom's* problems, whether imposed by politicians or of its own design. It is unable to look forward. In industries at the very centre of innovation the regulator is always looking backwards, incapable of a coherent and timely response to changes in the businesses it regulates. Anticipating the arrival of new technology is out of the question.

This conservatism is explicitly stated. "Investors need to know the environment in which they are operating will not change radically," it told the government back in 2011 as it explained its approach to economic regulation. "The market itself may develop and change, but the framework in which investment decisions are made should not."

A decade later, this creed seems ridiculous. For instance, the fundamental nature of the technological disruption in television has utterly changed the framework in which investment decisions are made. The global scale of streaming has transformed budgets for drama. Meanwhile the barriers to entry of broadcasting licensing are dissolved.

Change *Ofcom*'s modus operandi?

Ofcom and the laws that underpin it have not caught up. It needs a new approach which is faster and more flexible.

The best way to achieve this would be to change *Ofcom's* remit. It is currently duty-bound to work in the interests of consumers in only a very narrow sense that delivers low prices and choice. But in a market where the ground is shifting, consumers' interests can be served by more investment in broadband or by the rescue of public service broadcasting. With more broadly defined goals, *Ofcom* would have to develop new ways of thinking and working. Such a change would spark panic among those who still believe that regulation can be apolitical.

Ofcom as conceived in the Blair era, with the economic ideas that dominate its decision-making, was a political project that was already in need of reform by the time the phone hacking scandal arrived. The notion that those ideas are capable of responding to the online revolutions now well underway in the media and in telecoms - and those around the corner - is a fantasy. Fundamental renewal is required.

About the Contributor

Christopher Williams is the Business Editor of the *Telegraph*. He has held a series of senior posts at the paper including Technology, Media, and Telecoms Editor.

Bite-Sized Public Affairs Books

Bite-Sized Public Affairs Books are designed to provide insights and stimulating ideas that affect us all in, for example, journalism, social policy, education, government and politics.

They are deliberately short, easy to read, and authoritative books written by people who are either on the front line or who are informed observers. They are designed to stimulate discussion, thought and innovation in all areas of public affairs. They are all firmly based on personal experience and direct involvement and engagement.

The most successful people all share an ability to focus on what really matters, keeping things simple and understandable. When we are faced with a new challenge most of us need quick guidance on what matters most, from people who have been there before and who can show us where to start.

They can be read straight through at one easy sitting and then referred to as necessary – a trusted repository of hard-won experience.

BITE-SIZED BOOKS

Bite-Sized Books Catalogue

We publish Business Books, Life-Style Books, Public Affairs Books, including our BBC Books, Fiction – both short form and long form – and Children's Fiction. See our full range at https://bite-sizedbooks.com/